The Transforming Trinity

The Keswick Year Book 2013

The Transforming Trinity

Knowing the Triune God

Charles Price
John Risbridger
Paul Williams
Mike Hill
Paul Mallard
Richard Condie
Rico Tice
Peter Baker

First published 2014

British Library Cataloguing in Publication Data
A catalogue record for this book is available from the British Library.

ISBN: 978–1–78359–095–7
ePub: 978–1–78359–096–4
Mobi: 978–1–78359–097–1

Set in Dante 12.5/16pt
Typeset in Great Britain by CRB Associates, Potterhanworth, Lincolnshire
Printed and bound in Great Britain by Ashford Colour Press Ltd, Gosport, Hampshire

Contents

Introduction by the Chairman of the 2013 Convention

There is so much to savour as we look back on the 2013 Keswick Convention: the best Cumbrian summer for years, the record-breaking crowds filling the tent and overflow venues, and the stories of families and friends sharing the things they were learning across the generations. But at the heart of every Convention, there is one reality that outstrips all others in terms of its centrality and significance, and that is the sight of thousands of people of every age and from many backgrounds coming together to encounter the living God in the preaching of his Word, the praises of his people and the transforming presence of his Spirit.

The majesty and transformational power of this God was our central focus in the Convention this year, as we unpacked together the inspirational theme of *The*

Transforming Trinity. It wasn't just theory, however; the transforming Trinity was at work among us, bringing some to faith for the first time, renewing the faith of many others, and inspiring some to take the first steps in exploring God's calling to new expressions of Christian service and mission.

This Year Book will give you a taste of some of the most memorable teaching in the Convention. Alongside it, the *Transforming Trinity Study Guide* is an excellent resource to enable individuals and small groups to dig deeper into the central themes of the event – available on-line from thinkivp.com.

In addition to those who attended, thousands of others benefitted from the Convention through CDs, DVDs and digital downloads. So, if reading the Year Book leaves you wanting more, why not visit www.keswickministries.org, where you can find free downloads of the main talks, and the Essential Christian site, where you can purchase CDs and DVDs to access more of the Convention's ministry and share its blessings with others?

We hope you enjoy this reminder of Keswick 2013, and our prayer for you as you read it is that you will experience the transforming power of God in your own life.

John Risbridger
Chair, Keswick Ministries

The Bible Readings

The Diagnosing and Destroying of Spiritual Disease: Isaiah

by Charles Price

Charles Price has been the Senior Pastor of The Peoples Church in Toronto, Canada since September 2001. His television programme, *Living Truth*, is broadcast around the world. Charles came to Christ at the age of twelve and trained at Bible colleges in the UK, after two years farming in Zimbabwe. While on the staff of Capernwray Hall, he engaged in an itinerant ministry of evangelism and Bible teaching. Charles married Hilary in 1980, and they have three adult children.

1. The Diagnosis and Remedy of a Disease: Isaiah 1

There was once a couple where the husband became convinced that his wife was losing her hearing. She was equally convinced that she wasn't, and this became quite a point of tension between them. One day the husband decided to do a little experiment. He was standing in the kitchen, his wife was sitting in the lounge, and he asked, 'Would you like a cup of tea, dear?' There was no response, which was what he'd expected. He went into the passageway between the two rooms and he said again, 'Would you like a cup of tea, dear?' There was no response, and again he was not surprised. He stood right behind his wife and said, 'Would you like a cup of tea, dear?' And she said, 'For the third time, yes!'

In the book of Isaiah, God had a controversy with people, and people had a controversy with God. Chapter 3 says that their words and their deeds are against the Lord and against his glorious presence, and they felt that God was short-changing them.

A good prophet is like a good physician; he has two primary responsibilities: first of all to make an accurate diagnosis, and secondly to prescribe an effective remedy. I want to look with you at the diagnosis that Isaiah gives of the condition of the people of Israel. Not because we are curious about a bit of ancient history, but because the diagnosis he makes of their hearts is very likely a diagnosis that will be applicable to your heart and mine, because although times change and circumstances change, people don't. I want us to look with Dr Isaiah at three things that he summarizes in this first chapter: first of all he makes a diagnosis, then he looks at the symptoms and then he looks at the solution, the remedy that he is going to call them to.

They have forsaken the Lord

Let me talk first about Isaiah's diagnosis of the sickness. Isaiah 1:4b says, 'They have forsaken the LORD.' That is the summary of what is wrong with the people. There was a breakdown in their relationship with God. God's purpose for Israel was that they would experience and enjoy a relationship with him. In Isaiah 1:3 he says,

> The ox knows its master,
>   the donkey its owner's manger,

> but Israel does not know,
>   my people do not understand.

The ox knows its master, because every day he takes that ox out and works with it in the fields. The donkey is fed every day at its owner's manger. They know their owners by sheer familiarity. But God said to Isaiah that his people are not familiar with him: 'They take my name, they are known as the people of God, but they do not have an intimacy with me; they have lost familiarity with me.' And so he says,

> Your whole head is injured,
>   your whole heart afflicted.
> (verse 5)

When your head becomes detached from the truth about God, inevitably your heart becomes afflicted.

The heart of this dilemma is that the people 'have forsaken the LORD; they have spurned the Holy One of Israel and turned their backs on him' (verse 4). Now if you were to ask an Israelite, 'Why are you in this land?', they would probably say, 'Because God has privileged us with all the rich resources of this land of Cana.' And that would be partially true, but it would miss the essential point. In the first instance, God set his people apart for himself. He says this several times in the book of Isaiah. He speaks of them as 'the people I formed for myself' (Isaiah 43:21). The benefit of the milk and honey of the land is only a consequence. The whole enterprise was designed to bring the people to God. The initial diagnosis that Isaiah makes is that the Israelites have forsaken the Lord, the One who had brought them to himself. They have neglected him and forsaken him.

God seeks an active relationship with people. That was true for Israel under the old covenant, and under the new covenant it's true for his people today. In John 17:3 Jesus said, 'Now this is eternal life: that they may know you, the only true God, and Jesus Christ, whom you have sent.' The word 'know' involves not just some intellectual appreciation of him, but experience of him. Paul wrote in Philippians 3:10: 'I want to know Christ [experimentally] – yes, to know the power of his resurrection.' Paul prays for the Ephesian Christians, 'I keep asking that the God of our Lord Jesus Christ, the glorious Father, may give you the Spirit of wisdom and revelation, so that you may know him better' (Ephesians 1:17). The Christian life is not defined by our creed, although that is necessary, nor by our experiences, although those are valid, nor by our activities, though they may be good. It's defined in the first instance by an active, developing relationship with God himself, where you actually connect and commune with him. The most subtle temptation for us in the Christian life is to get so caught up in the things of God that we lose God himself.

I was going through a difficult time a while ago, and a number of symptoms of the pressure I was under were manifesting themselves. My wife Hilary said to me, 'Is Jesus your friend?' I thought for a moment and said, 'Well, I know he is my business partner: I work with him; most of my dealings have to do with him; I am concerned to know his Word, his will and his power, but I am not sure if he is my friend.' And Hilary said, 'I can see that. Make him your friend.' It was a very challenging word to me. I actually cancelled some things and took those days to go away on my own and seek to re-establish friendship with God himself.

You know, we cannot live the Christian life without developing a relationship with God. The question, 'Have you come to know Christ?', is not a good enough question. You might answer in the affirmative: 'Yes, I came to know Christ twenty years ago.' But the real question is: 'Do you know him? Are you experiencing him?' We talk about a relationship with God as the lingo of Christianity, but I am utterly convinced that many people do not have a relationship with him at all. So, when they face a crisis in their life, they don't have resources. And the person next door who never darkens a church, who plays golf on a Sunday, is just as able to cope as the person who says, 'I know Christ.'

Sometimes when I conduct a wedding, I talk about togetherness in marriage. I will say there are two kinds of togetherness in a marriage: a side-by-side togetherness where you are moving together through life, and a face-to-face togetherness which is just about the two of you. Sometimes we become so occupied with the side-by-side togetherness. We are busy, we have jobs, we have a family, we are looking after the house and we have little or no time for face-to-face togetherness. In fact, when we do turn and look at each other, we realize that we don't really know each other any more. Our hearts are not open to each other, we are not vulnerable together and we don't feed into each other. I say to a newly married couple, 'Whatever you do, make time for face-to-face togetherness.' This is what happened to the Israelites; it's what happened to me. We become so busy in good things, but we lose touch with God himself. And so, in verse 4 God says, 'They have forsaken the LORD; they have spurned the Holy One of Israel and turned their backs on him.' Notice that the face-to-face posture has become a back-to-back posture, and the consequences are that they have broken fellowship with God.

Stop bringing meaningless offerings

Secondly, let's look at the symptoms. Verses 13 and 15 are key verses here:

> Stop bringing meaningless offerings! . . .
> When you spread out your hands in prayer,
>   I hide my eyes from you;
> even when you offer many prayers,
>   I am not listening.

These are remarkable statements that God is making to the people. It was God who initiated the sacrificial system. When men, women, boys and girls recognized their need to be reconciled to God, they were to bring bulls, lambs and rams to the tabernacle to atone for their sins. God had initiated this, but he says, 'I am sick of your offerings.' Every ritual that God inaugurated for Israel never stood as an end in itself. When a man brought his lamb for sacrifice, the reality he was acknowledging was his sin, and his need to be forgiven and restored to a relationship with God. On the part of the priest who represented God in the temple, or previously in the tabernacle, the ritual represented the reality of God's need for atonement; sin had to be paid for.

Now we know from the New Testament that the blood of bulls, lambs and goats could never remove sin; it could only cover it. It was only the blood of Christ that removed sin. What is the difference? I think the difference is that the blood of animals was like a cheque. A cheque is a worthless piece of paper. There is no intrinsic value in a cheque; there is only value in as much as the cheque corresponds to the cash that is in the bank on the account that the cheque is written. But supposing I wanted to make a purchase and I haven't got enough money in my account. I come to an arrangement with the person I'm making the purchase from and post-date the cheque to the first of the month. I write the value of the purchase on the cheque and post-date it to the first of next month. I hand over the cheque and he hands me the goods. The debt is covered, but it is not removed until there is cash in the bank on the first of the month. And so, the blood of bulls and goats was like worthless cheques that had no intrinsic value, but were post-dated 'Calvary'. So, when Jesus Christ on the cross cried out, 'It is finished', the message that went back through the corridors of history was: 'There is cash in the bank; exchange your cheques!' And every man, woman, boy and girl who brought an animal in sacrifice on behalf of their sin was forgiven on the basis of the only currency that has validity, which is the blood of Jesus Christ himself.

Now the point is that these people were bringing the blood of bulls and goats, and God says to them, 'It's meaningless. I hate your sacrifices.' And the reason is because the ritual had become detached from the reality to which it was pointed. When a ritual becomes detached from the reality, the ritual replaces the reality, and the all-important thing becomes the ritual itself. 'As long as I have offered the sacrifice, it doesn't matter whether I am repentant or not, whether I could care less about God or not. I've done it.' The ritual becomes the end product in itself.

I'll illustrate this. We don't have rituals in the New Testament, but we have some symbols which have been given to us by Jesus. In communion, the symbol is the bread speaking of his body, the wine speaking of his blood. The ritual is the eating and drinking of it, but the reality to which it points is Christ himself: 'Do this in remembrance of me. Do this to remind yourselves that the only grounds on which it is possible for you to be reconciled with God is the broken body and shed blood of Jesus Christ.' But supposing someone doesn't know Jesus Christ, supposing they are not concerned about being reconciled with God. Can they still participate in communion? Yes, they can, but I can tell what will happen. Instead of the ritual pointing to the reality, the ritual will replace the reality. The all-important thing will not be 'I have remembered him', but 'I had it', and we become superstitious about it.

When I became a Christian, I was told that I should read my Bible every day, which was very good advice, but no-one told me why. I began to think that the reason I should read my Bible was to get another Bible. But then I discovered that Jesus criticized people for reading their Bible: 'You study the Scriptures diligently because you think that in them you have eternal life. These are the very Scriptures that testify about me, yet you refuse to come to me to have life' (John 5:39–40). If you study the Bible to get another Bible, it makes you a Pharisee. Jesus said, 'Study the Bible to get to know me.' The ritual of reading the Word of God, vital as that is, becomes a problem unless beyond the written word we are looking to, and engaging with, the Living Word.

I have a Toyota Camry at home. When I got my Toyota, there was an instruction manual with it. I read the instruction manual not because I wanted to know all about the instruction manual; I had a better reason – I wanted to know all about the car. Now, of course, I could have read the instruction manual a little bit every night before I went to bed. I could have underlined the bits that I liked. I could have memorized my favourite parts. I could have put it to music and sung it. I could have joined the local Toyota fellowship and gone every week for an exposition of the manual – this week's subject: 'Spark plugs'. If I was a fanatic, I could have studied Japanese to read the manual in the original language. But having read the manual, memorized it, put it to music, sung it, joined the fellowship, studied Japanese, I would still get bored with the manual. Why? Because the manual has one purpose: that I might know the car.

The purpose of the written Word of God is that through the written Word we know and engage with the Living Word and we know Jesus Christ better. As the words of a hymn we used to sing remind us, 'Beyond the sacred page I seek Thee, Lord.' What happened here in Isaiah 1 is that the rituals have become substitutes for the realities, and so God says, 'I have no pleasure in the blood of bulls and lambs and goats . . . Stop bringing meaningless offerings' (Isaiah 1:13, 15).

There is a second symptom, which we don't have time to talk about because the clock is going too quickly: it's about stopping doing wrong and learning to do right. Isaiah talks about the ethical outworking, because the true evidence of a genuine relationship with God is the way we behave. Jesus said, 'By this everyone will know that you are my disciples, if you love one another' (John 13:35). Francis Schaeffer said that Jesus Christ gave the world the right to test the legitimacy to anybody's claim to be a Christian not by their doctrine, but by their love.

Come now, let us reason together

I need to come to the third point, which is the solution. What's the solution? What's the medication that Isaiah is able to apply? Well, verse 18 says, '"Come now, let us reason together" says the LORD.'[1] Earlier, God says, 'You have turned your backs' (verse 4). Now he is inviting them to turn their face towards him. And he says, 'Let's talk, let's reason, let's chat, let's discuss, let's listen.' 'Come to me' is the invitation. You know, we cannot outsource our spiritual lives. We outsource many aspects of our lives: we might outsource the handling of our finances and taxes by getting an accountant; we might outsource our legal issues by getting a lawyer; we might outsource our medical issues by getting a doctor; but you cannot outsource your spiritual life to your pastor, your minister or your church. You might think, 'If I turn up, they'll have done the hard work and that will simply rub off on me.' But there comes a time in your Christian life when the depth of it, the quality of it and the integrity of it are only possible when, as Jesus said, you go into your room, close the door and deal with God in secret, deal with him personally, deal with him directly (Matthew 6:6).

On Sunday mornings at the church that I serve, there is usually a line of people who are going to want to talk to me about something or other after the sermon. One Sunday morning not long ago, after about thirty minutes talking to other people, I got to this man in the line. I said, 'How can I help you?' He said, 'I'd like you to pray for me. I have an interview tomorrow for a job that I would really like to get. Would you pray that I will get that job?' I said, 'Have you been lining up for thirty minutes to ask me to do that?' He said, 'Yes'. I said, 'Why didn't you ask the person next to you to pray with you when you were sitting in the seats?' He said, 'Because I want you to pray for me. You are the minister, so I think it would be better if you prayed.' I said, 'You know, if I pray for you I will perpetrate your spiritual immaturity. I am sorry to be direct, but I don't have any access to God that you don't have.' I said, 'I will pray for you because you have been waiting for thirty minutes, but what we will do is this: you will pray, and I'll say the biggest "Amen" at the end of your prayer, but that will be my sole contribution.' He said, 'I don't know how to pray.' I said, 'Now you are talking about the real issue. Why don't you know how to pray?' He said, 'I don't know. I'm just too busy.' I said, 'As long as you come running to people like me, you'll never know God for yourself. You'll never know what it is to experience his presence and go out in the morning with that quiet confidence that, whatever happens in the course of the day, you can trust God.'

We can't outsource our spiritual lives. You know, it's great you are here at Keswick, but you can't come to Keswick to put your battery on charge and hope it will survive for the next fifty-one weeks. His mercies are new every morning, and his invitation is: 'Come to me, let us reason together.' This is by the by, but I think if we get hold of these four invitations of Jesus, we will have got hold of much of the Christian life: Come to me; abide in me; learn of me; follow me. Jesus says, 'If you come to me, I'll give you rest. In other words, I'll take your burdens' (Matthew 11:28). 'If you abide in me I'll give you fruit. If you will learn of me I'll place my yoke on your shoulders.' A yoke is what you put on two oxen. And if one is stronger, older or more experienced than the other, you adjust the yoke in such a way that they walk together evenly, one taking more of the burden than the other. Jesus says, 'If you come to me, I'll put my yoke on your shoulders. My yoke is easy, my burden is light, but you'll learn of me and what that means is you say, "Lord, I am not just here for you to bless me; I'm here to work with you. What do you want me to do?"' And then Jesus says, 'Follow me.' He says that several times of course, but the first time he said, 'Follow me and I'll make you fishers of men.'

So, the cry God gives through Isaiah to the people is here: 'Come, let us reason together.' And he says, 'If you come back to me, there are three things you'll come back to me for. First of all, you'll come to me for cleansing.' Verse 18 says,

> Though your sins are like scarlet,
>   they shall be as white as snow;
> though they are red as crimson,
>   they shall be like wool.

Our dealings with God always begin with forgiveness and cleansing. We come not just for cleansing; we come to him for chastisement – for correction, in other words. Verses 19–20 say,

> 'If you are willing and obedient,
>   you will eat the good things of the land;

> but if you resist and rebel,
> you will be devoured by the sword.'
> For the mouth of the LORD has spoken.

And in verse 25:

> I will turn my hand against you;
> I will thoroughly purge away your dross
> and remove all your impurities.

'So, you've got to come to me for cleansing. It's not just a wash; it is going to be a purging; it's going to involve chastisement. The book of Hebrews says, "God chastises those he loves." I am going to go deep into the guts of your problem, and we are going to work it out together.' That will involve his moulding us, disciplining us, smoothing the rough parts of us, and I am sure many of you know the discipline of God in your life. We often recognize it more easily in retrospect. We see how God has taken us into things that we would have avoided at all cost, but in so doing, he has brought about not just a cleansing, but a purifying. Thirdly, we come to God for commission. In verse 26, he says,

> I will restore your leaders as in days of old,
> your rulers as at the beginning.
> Afterwards you will be called
> the City of Righteousness,
> the Faithful City.

What a turnaround! God says, 'You people who have turned away from me, I hate your sacrifice, I hate the blood of bulls and goats, and if you pray, I won't listen to you.' But now he says, 'Here is what's possible. You will be called the City of Righteousness, the Faithful City. You see, when I cleanse you, correct and chastise you, I will commission you again to be the means by which my character, my righteousness, is going to be seen in people's lives.'

There is an old hymn that says,

I've wandered far away from God,
Now I'm coming home;
The paths of sin too long I've trod,
Lord, I'm coming home.

Coming home, coming home,
Nevermore to roam;
Open wide Thine arms of love,
Lord, I'm coming home.[2]

Will that be your prayer this morning?

Notes

1. ESV.
2. William J. Kirkpatrick, 'Lord, I'm Coming Home' (1892).

2. A Transforming Experience of God: Isaiah 6

Back at home I pulled a book off my shelf entitled *They Found the Secret*[1] by Raymond Edman, who was the President of Wheaton College. The subtitle of this book was: *Twenty Transformed Lives.* It is a series of short biographies of Christian leaders who came to a point in their lives of utter despair about themselves and their own abilities, and at that time they met with God in a totally new way. Some of the people in that book will be well known to us: Hudson Taylor who founded what is now the Overseas Missionary Fellowship; William Booth who founded the Salvation Army; Amy Carmichael who was the first missionary sent out by the Keswick Convention and went to India. They had all come to know Christ, become enthusiastic about the Christian life, begun to serve God in various ways, and in almost every instance, they became burnt out in the process. And in that time of despair they had a fresh encounter with God. They found a rest, an empowering, a new awareness of God in their lives, and they became fruitful in ways they had never been before.

Isaiah is in that long line of people who have been through something of that nature. In Isaiah 6, he has already been ministering for five chapters, but he had an encounter with God that transformed his life. He dates it in the first verse: 'In the year that King Uzziah died, I saw the Lord, high and exalted, seated on a throne; and the train of his robe filled the temple.' Now it is very likely that the reference to the death of King Uzziah is not merely dating the event, but that the event itself precipitated Isaiah's vision of God.

An obstacle that had to be removed

The first point I want to make is that there was an obstacle that had to be removed for Isaiah to see God. Turn to 2 Chronicles 26, because I think it's important to understand a bit about King Uzziah. He was a great king: 'His fame spread far and wide, for he was greatly helped until he became powerful. But after Uzziah became powerful, his pride led to his downfall. He was unfaithful to the LORD his God, and entered the temple of the LORD to burn incense on the altar of incense' (2 Chronicles 26:15–16). Only priests were permitted to do that, and in his pride as a successful king on whose life had been the anointing and enabling of God, he had developed a sense of entitlement, which is always a danger for a leader. He'd gone into the temple to offer incense when he had no right to do that, and eighty brave priests confronted him. Uzziah was angry, and as he was in the middle of this rage, leprosy broke out on his forehead. Verse 21 says, 'King Uzziah had leprosy until the day he died. He lived in a separate house – leprous, and excluded from the temple of the LORD.'

Now I give you all this background because I suggest that Uzziah had become a blockage to Isaiah seeing God for himself. Verse 1 says, 'In the year that King Uzziah died, I saw the Lord . . . seated on a throne.' When Uzziah was on the throne, he had eclipsed Isaiah's vision of God, but now that King Uzziah has died, his vision is cleared and he sees the Lord seated on the throne. I suggest to you two possible reasons for this. First, Isaiah may have been mesmerized by Uzziah. Perhaps he looked to him as a spiritual leader, one who listened to God and demonstrated the presence of God in his life for most of his reign. And maybe, as a result, Isaiah had been looking to Uzziah and had not been looking directly to God.

It is right, of course, that we look to leaders whom God raises up. In Hebrews 13:7, the writer says, 'Remember your leaders, who spoke the word of God to you. Consider the outcome of their way of life and imitate their faith.' Notice it says, 'Consider your leaders': consider what makes them tick and the outcome of their life, but don't imitate their behaviour; imitate their faith, imitate their trust in God. But sometimes we don't do that; we look to the leader, we depend upon that leader, and our dealings with God come through that person, and God himself becomes eclipsed by that person.

I don't want to be controversial about this, but a wife can look to her husband as her spiritual leader, and not be dealing with God directly. A man can look to his wife as the more spiritual one of the two, and not be dealing with God directly. Some people look to their church or to a leader whom they respect and admire, and there is nothing wrong with that, but they have no real discernment of their own about the things of God; they are looking to this other person.

Maybe Isaiah was mesmerized by Uzziah. Maybe it was the opposite; maybe Isaiah was disillusioned by Uzziah. Perhaps he did know that his leprosy was a result of his pride and God's judgment on him. Maybe he had become disappointed with this man of God to whom he had looked, and his confidence had been shaken. I know it can be an awful thing when someone you respect and trust suddenly falls. We are totally confused, our boat begins to rock and we become insecure and uncertain.

So Isaiah may have been mesmerized by Uzziah; he might have been disillusioned by Uzziah. But I attach significance to this, because it's when Uzziah died and was no longer on the throne that Isaiah saw the Lord seated in the place where Uzziah had been. I ask you this morning, what is it that intercepts your vision of God? Where in your Christian life are you a second-hand receiver of the grace of God? Of course, we need the benefit of ministering to one another, we need fellowship; we don't go into isolation and deal only with God. But you will know if your relationship with God is real by what happens when you suddenly face a crisis, and find whether God is sufficient for you or not.

An awareness that had to be renewed

There is an awareness that had to be renewed in this process. First of all, Isaiah had a renewed awareness of God: 'I saw the Lord seated on the throne.' Now John tells us in his Gospel that no-one has seen God at any time, so Isaiah didn't see a physical God on the throne. John 12:41 tells us that Isaiah saw Jesus' glory. He saw a representation of the glory of God, and there are a number of things described for us here. God was on a throne, a seat of sovereignty, authority and power; he was high and exalted – he saw him in his position of supremacy; there were seraphs above him who were in the position of servants attending to him. Seraphs or seraphim are a species of angel. There are different kinds of angels in Scripture, and this is the only time that seraphs appear in the Bible. They have six wings: with two they were covering their faces, with two they were covering their feet, and with two they were flying. And as they encircled this throne, they were calling to one another,

> Holy, holy, holy is the LORD Almighty;
> the whole earth is full of his glory.
> (Isaiah 6:3)

Everything they were doing and saying was pointing to God, pointing to his glory.

At the same time, there is an atmosphere of confusion, uncertainty, even fear. 'At the sound of their voices the doorposts and thresholds shook and the temple was filled with smoke' (verse 4). It sounds like a rock concert! Everything is shaking, the volume is high and the building is filled with smoke. We have the grandeur of God on his throne, and then you've got this chaos because God fits no earthly paradigm. There is nothing to which we can compare God. The revelation here is both wonderful and confusing; it's terrific and terrifying. In Isaiah 46:5 God asks,

> To whom will you compare me or count me equal?
>   To whom will you liken me that we may be compared?

The answer is: 'No-one'. And so God settles for these graphic images that are both wonderful and confusing. Don't pin God down to be so predictable and so definable that you are never able to see when he might do something out of the ordinary.

Isaiah has a renewed awareness of God and also a renewed awareness of himself. '"Woe to me!" I cried. "I am ruined! For I am a man of unclean lips, and I live among a people of unclean lips, and my eyes have seen the King, the LORD Almighty"' (verse 5). Now notice that Isaiah's 'Woe to me! I am ruined! I am a man of unclean lips' is because 'I have seen the LORD.' That is significant; we don't see ourselves truthfully until we have a revelation of God. When we see God and his holiness, we recognize our unholiness. You see, we can only understand sin in the light of understanding God. The word 'sin' means 'to miss the mark'. I understand that it was originally used in archery. You took an arrow and fired it at a target; if you missed the target it was called 'sin'. If you missed by half an inch it was called sin; if you missed by half a foot it was called sin; if you missed by half a yard it was called sin; if you shoot in the opposite direction it's called sin. Sin is not a measurement of how bad we are; it's a measurement of how good we are not. If you miss a bus by a minute you've missed it; if you miss by five minutes you've missed it, miss by thirty minutes you've missed it. You don't congratulate yourself when you miss a bus by a minute: 'That was fantastic – I only missed it by a minute today.' You know, God is not particularly concerned with how bad we are; he is concerned with how good we are.

If sin is to miss the mark, it means that sin is a relative word. We do not know what sin is unless we know what mark we've missed. So what is the mark? Romans 3:23 says, 'For all have sinned and fall short of the glory of God.' The glory of God is the moral character of God; it is the beauty of God. What Isaiah sees in this vision is the glory of God. And as he sees the glory of God, he sees what he is not morally, so his inevitable response is: 'Woe to me!' That's why of course we don't preach sin to people; we preach Christ to people, and when people see Christ, they see their sin.

It was very interesting on the day of Pentecost when Peter preached. Do you remember his sermon that day, talking about the whole earthly career of Jesus leading to his exultation to the right hand of the Father? 'When the people heard this, they were cut to the heart and said to Peter and the other apostles, "Brothers, what shall we do?"' (Acts 2:37). I find that very interesting, because Peter hadn't told them that they could do anything. He wasn't talking about them; he was talking about Christ. But the effect of talking about Christ is that the people suddenly said, 'What do we do?', because in seeing Christ we've seen ourselves.

When a person meets God, they never become cocky – they are humble in the realization: 'Woe is me!' When Job had gone through that awful experience, he said,

> My ears had heard of you
> but now my eyes have seen you.
> (Job 42:5)

There is a big difference between your ears hearing and your eyes seeing. Job was saying, 'My doctrinal i's were dotted and my t's were crossed. I knew it, I'd heard it, I understood it, I believed it, but now I've seen God.' And then he says,

> Therefore, I despise myself
> and repent in dust and ashes.
> (verse 6)

'I've seen him and therefore I realize my own true nature.' Humility is not an add-on to the Christian life; humility is always a consequence of the Christian life, when you realize yourself, in the light of the glory of Jesus Christ, the glory that we have come short of. The more we know him, the more God makes us aware of our sin – not to humiliate us, not to embarrass us, not to condemn us, not to rub our nose in our own dirt – he makes us aware of our sin that he might clean us up, transform us. When a person meets with God, his response is always that humble response: 'Woe to me!'

Now I want you to notice the effect that this has on Isaiah. He's already been preaching for five chapters. Let me read to you some things that he has been saying: Isaiah 5:8 says,

> Woe to you who add house to house
> 　and join field to field
> till no space is left.

In verse 11 he says,

> Woe to those who rise early in the morning
> 　to run after their drinks.

In verse 18 he says, 'Woe to those who draw sin along with cords of deceit.' He says in verse 20, 'Woe to those who call evil good and good evil.' In verse 21 he says, 'Woe to those who are wise in their own eyes.' In verse 22 he says, 'Woe to those who are heroes at drinking wine and champions at mixing drinks.' Isaiah's message on the streets of Jerusalem is: 'Woe to you, woe to them, woe to you, woe to them'. And then in chapter 6 he meets God, and his message changes: 'Woe to me! I am a man of unclean lips.' You know, the 'Woe to them' message is usually the message of folks who have a clear understanding of right and wrong, truth and error, but they have never been broken before God. When a man sees God, he speaks only out of his brokenness. And Isaiah later does say, 'Woe to them' about other things, but it's out of brokenness, an awareness of his own sin.

God exposed Isaiah's failure and his sin not to humiliate or condemn him; God always exposes our sin that he might liberate us. So in verse 6 he says, 'Then one of the seraphs flew to me with a live coal in his hand, which he had taken with tongs from the altar. With it he touched my mouth and said, "See, this has touched your lips; your guilt is taken away and your sin atoned for."' There is nothing as marvellous as knowing that we have been cleansed, especially when you know the condition of your own heart. It would seem that Isaiah's sin had to do with his mouth. He says in verse 5, 'I am a man of unclean lips', and in verse 7, 'He touched my mouth and said, "See this has touched your lips; your guilt is taken away."' It seems that Isaiah's sin was his lips. I wonder if his sin hadn't been his ministry: 'Woe to them, woe to them, woe to them'. What he said is true. Isaiah 5 is the inspired Word of God, inerrant and deriving from God himself, so we don't doubt the authenticity of what he is saying. But I think the challenge is the spirit in which he's been saying it, and so his mouth, his lips have to be cleansed.

You know, our lips and our sins are very connected. 'For the mouth speaks what the heart is full of.' The lips become the barometer of what's going on inside (Luke 6:45). And you know, along with that, the only way sin ever leaves your body is through your mouth. 'If we confess our sins, he is faithful and just and will forgive us our sins and purify us from all unrighteousness' (1 John 1:9). 'If we confess our sins' doesn't mean that we have to remember every sin we have ever committed, because that would be impossible. But in allowing our lips to verbalize, 'Woe to me!', we are confessing before God. Notice the very area of his sin, which has been his mouth and lips, is the area in which he is commissioned and becomes his ministry: 'Go and tell this people' (verse 9).

A direction to be reviewed

There was an obstacle that had to be removed, an awareness that had to be renewed and thirdly a direction to be reviewed. In verse 8 the Lord asks, 'Whom shall I send? And who will go for us?' That's interesting, because I think Isaiah is having this vision of God alone. Normally, those deep life-changing encounters with God take place in solitude. There is only Isaiah here, but you know, the Lord Jesus is a good shepherd. An eastern shepherd goes in front of his sheep: 'He goes on ahead of them, and his sheep follow him because they know his voice' (John 10:4). Now he's not saying, 'Isaiah, I've backed you into a corner. You'd better go.' You are no use until you say from your heart, as Isaiah said from his heart, 'Here am I. Send me!' (verse 8). Don't be frogmarched into Christian service; come for one reason alone: you love the Lord Jesus Christ and you sense his calling. I've been to enough mission fields to know that the biggest problem is missionaries who shouldn't be there. Wait for God to call you, to lead you. 'Who will go for me?' And Isaiah's answer is: 'Here am I. Send me!' His cleansed mouth becomes the means of his ministry.

Henri Nouwen explained that nobody escapes being wounded. We are all wounded – physically, emotionally, mentally or spiritually. The main question is not how can we hide our wounds, but how can we use our woundedness in the service of God and others. When our wounds cease to be a source of shame and become a source of healing, we have become wounded healers. Isaiah has had his sin exposed, the shame of his lips exposed. Now God says, 'Your area of woundedness, your area of sin, is to become your area of ministry.' That's why again and again, when we have fallen in some area, when we've gone through experiences we wished we would not have had to go through, those become the very means by which God blesses other people through our lives.

I was at a conference about two summers ago in Japan. I was there to speak that week and I was having a meal with somebody and said, 'Why are there so many German missionaries in Japan?' He said, 'You know, at the end of the war the American church said, "Now is the time to evangelize Japan." General MacArthur actually called for Bibles to be shipped to Japan in their millions. When these American missionaries came into Japan to evangelize the defeated nation, the dignity of the Japanese people, which makes them very conscious of shame, meant they couldn't look those American missionaries in the eye. They felt inferior, because they were a defeated people and the Americans were the conquerors. Most of the American missionaries went home saying, "It's a very hard place; we can't get anywhere." Meanwhile, the church in Germany said, "Where are we going to send our missionaries? The world hates us. There is only one place; let's send them to Japan." And the Japanese welcomed them as people on the same level, a defeated nation.'

German missions in those post-war years had a huge effect that American missions did not. And three generations later there is still a high proportion of German missionaries in Japan. God took the humiliation of the war, the pain the German nation went through, and in the Christian people he redeemed it and made it a blessing. You know, our past failures, our sins, our experiences of life are the quarry from which God digs our ministry. We don't have to give everybody all the details about our lives, but people know when you are authentic and they know when you are not; they know when it's words and they know when it's life, because it comes out of that brokenness that is so often painful, but which God leads us through.

But you know, Isaiah was sent to a ministry of failure. I think his commission is probably the most frustrating assignment ever given to anybody at any time. Let me read verses 9–10:

> Go and tell this people:
>
> 'Be ever hearing, but never understanding;
> be ever seeing, but never perceiving.'
> Make the heart of this people calloused;
> make their ears dull
> and close their eyes.
> Otherwise they might see with their eyes,
> hear with their ears,
> understand with their hearts,
> and turn and be healed.

And Isaiah asks, 'For how long, O Lord?' God answers:

> Until the cities lie ruined
> and without inhabitant,
> until the houses are left deserted
> and the fields ruined and ravaged,
> until the LORD has sent everyone far away
> and the land is utterly forsaken.
> And though a tenth remains in the land
> it will again be laid waste.
> But as the terebinth and oak
> leave stumps when they are cut down,
> so the holy seed will be the stump in the land.
> (verses 11–13)

You see, your ministry and your life are not just about the three score years and ten that you're here. God is working for the long period; he has a wonderful plan for your life, but it might be a terrible process. 'Isaiah, you are never going to go home at night and say, "That was a fantastic service. So many people came to know God – we are really growing in leaps and bounds." You'll go home every night and say, "What a waste of time." But Isaiah, you are sowing seeds, history has a course and out of your ministry will come not only the reassurance about what God is going to do in those dark days of Judah's exile, but Isaiah, you are going to leave behind a book of sixty-six chapters. It's going to be read in 2,800 years time at the Keswick Convention. So relax, Isaiah, you are going to have a ministry, but you won't see it. Be content with the source of your ministry.' You know, anybody can fulfil a ministry that is successful. It takes a man whose security is in God alone to fulfil a ministry that is not successful in the human, visible, here-and-now sense.

God then describes the nation as a forest where all the trees are cut down. In the Sequoia National Park in California, there is Stump Meadow – acres and acres of dead stumps of redwood trees that were chopped down thirty or forty years ago. It looks like a graveyard, but every once in a while in one of those stumps there's a green branch coming out. And that's the picture Isaiah gives in verse 13. Ninety per cent of the people are going to go off into exile and ten per cent will stay. This nation will look devastated and chopped down like Stump Meadow, but there is going to be a holy seed that will come out of the stump. Isaiah 11:1 says,

> A shoot will come up from the stump of Jesse;
> from his roots a Branch will bear fruit.

This, of course, is a messianic statement about Christ: from the stump has come this shoot, and the Spirit of God will be upon him.

This is God's agenda for the nation of Judah, but in our own lives and our own circumstances when things go so tragically wrong, when things blind-side us and we cannot see the hand of God in them, be patient and trust him, because the principle is that out of the stump will come shoots. In this case it's going to be the Messiah, but it's a principle for your life as well. Some of the most horrendous things that have taken place in our lives, things we wish we'd never experienced, will be taken by the incredible love and grace of God and moulded into something beautiful and become a blessing to others. Some of you know that in your own lives. Isaiah was to learn that, but the big picture is that from all those broken-down stumps will come a shoot, and the Spirit of God will be on him.

Note

1. Raymond Edman, *They Found the Secret* (Zondervan, 1960, 1984).

3. The Holy Spirit's Active Ministry: Isaiah 11

I want to talk about the Holy Spirit in the life of Jesus, given to us here in Isaiah 11. There is a more explicit revelation of Christ, God the Son, in Isaiah than in any other of the Old Testament prophets. The crescendo comes in the Servant Songs in Isaiah chapters 42, 49, 50 and 53, but in the early part of Isaiah there is a series of teasers that are clearly leading us to this revelation of the Messiah, the hope of Israel and the world. Let me just show you one or two of those clues. Isaiah 7:14 says, 'Therefore the Lord himself will give you a sign: The virgin will . . . give birth to a son, and will call him Immanuel.' This is a familiar text from our Carols by Candlelight services. Isaiah is addressing King Ahaz, but we recognize there is a much fuller meaning behind this. In fact, the Gospel of Matthew says, 'All this took place to fulfil what the Lord had said through the prophet', and he quotes this verse (Matthew 1:22–23). So here is the teaser: there is going to be a child, born to a virgin, whose name will be Immanuel, which means 'God with us'. In Isaiah 9:6 we have another statement:

> To us a child is born,
> to us a son is given,
> and the government will be on his shoulders.
> And he will be called
> Wonderful Counsellor, Mighty God.

And in 11:1–2 it says,

> A shoot will come up from the stump of Jesse;
> from his roots a Branch will bear fruit.
> The Spirit of the LORD will rest on him.

So these are three major pointers that Isaiah gives about Jesus. Who is he? Immanuel, God with us. What will he do? The government will be on his shoulders. How will he do it? The Spirit of the Lord will rest on him.

I want to look at this last aspect with you now, not only because we are interested in the role of the Holy Spirit in the life of Jesus, which is a fascinating subject, but also because Jesus Christ in his humanity is the prototype of what redeemed men and women will be, having been reconciled to God and indwelt by his Holy Spirit. Jesus therefore is a prototype of the life you and I have been called to live. Jesus of course was a perfect man, but he was a real man. He wasn't simply God disguised as a man; he wasn't simply pretending to be a man. He wasn't lying in that manger in Bethlehem, saying to himself, 'Any minute now the wise men should be appearing.' He became a real man; he grew in wisdom and in favour with God and men. He had to learn things by what he suffered.

He is described by Paul in 1 Corinthians 15 as being the 'second man' and the 'last Adam'. What does it mean that he was the 'second man'? Surely Cain, the first-born son of Adam, was the second man in history? But Paul is saying that Jesus is the second man as God intended human beings to be. When he had created Adam in the first instance, his intention was that humanity would live in communion with God, indwelt by the Spirit of God. In the garden of Eden, God said to Adam and Eve, 'You can do whatever you like except one thing: don't eat of the tree of the knowledge of good and evil, for the day you eat of it you will die.' Well, when they ate it, did they die? When God came into the garden in the cool of the day, did he find two corpses under the tree? No, they didn't die physically, but they did die spiritually. In the words of Paul in Ephesians 4:18, 'They are . . . separated from the life of God.' That is the nature of spiritual death.

There was a time in your life when you were physically alive, but you were separated from the life of God. You were spiritually dead and therefore ill-equipped to live as you were designed to live. But the Lord Jesus, as the second man, as God intended man to be, was radically different. John 1:4 explains, 'In him was life, and that life was the light of all mankind.' In him was this quality that Adam had lost: spiritual life, the life of God. It was this life that is the light of men, this life that switches people on. Therefore, when we look at the Spirit of the Lord resting upon this one he describes as 'the Branch from the stump of Jesse', we are looking at what is intended for those of us who have been reconciled to God and indwelt by the Holy Spirit. Therefore, in Jesus we see the model of true humanity. That's why we say the goal of the Christian life is that we are increasingly like Jesus. What is true of him increasingly becomes true of us. Not to the level of perfection, because God has not made provision for that in this life. The flesh, the old nature, will constantly fight against the Spirit and keep us from doing what is right. Scripture makes it clear that there will come a day when we are liberated from this body of death and we will be fully restored in his image. Having been processed from one degree of glory to another in this life, we will then be glorified and made fully like Christ. But in the meantime, the work of the Spirit that is described here in the life of Jesus is the work of the Spirit increasingly making us the people we are designed to be.

The Spirit of the Lord will rest upon him

Let's look at the first point in verse 2: 'The Spirit of the LORD will rest on him' – he will be indispensable to the human life of Jesus. In his book *Mere Christianity*,[1] C. S. Lewis explained that, just as a car is made to run on petrol and would not run properly on anything else, so God designed the human machine to run on himself. He himself is the fuel our spirits were designed to burn; there is no other fuel. God cannot give us happiness and peace apart from himself, because there is no such thing. God created human beings to function in dependence on the Spirit of God, as we create a combustion engine to run on petrol. If there is no petrol, the car doesn't go very far; if there is no Spirit of God, we malfunction. Paul says that if a man does not have the Spirit of God, he does not belong to him. That doesn't mean that you receive the Holy Spirit when you become a Christian. It's the reverse: you become a Christian when you receive the Holy Spirit, because his very presence gives us life. When I became a Christian, I received only one thing. God had only one thing to give me – he gave me himself. The source of the Christian life is the indwelling presence of Jesus Christ by the Holy Spirit. The life of Jesus, the prototype of the Christian life, is a life lived by the Spirit of God, and your life is lived out of that indwelling presence of the Holy Spirit.

It says in Colossians 2:9, 'For in Christ all the fulness of the Deity lives in bodily form, and you have been given fulness in Christ.' Of course, there is a trinitarian aspect to this: if you read Ephesians 3:19, it talks about 'being filled to the measure of all the fulness of God'; Ephesians 4:13 talks about 'attaining to the whole measure of the fulness of Christ'; Ephesians 5:18 says, 'Do not get drunk on wine, which leads to debauchery. Instead, be filled with the Spirit.' So in chapter 3 you've got the fullness of God, in chapter 4 the fullness of Christ, and in chapter 5 the fullness of the Holy Spirit. These are not three different fullnesses; it's a trinitarian fullness. The Holy Spirit who lives within us is the life of Christ and shows us the work of God.

Last night Alasdair Paine talked about the two dimensions of our salvation: Christ for us and the Holy Spirit in us. One leads to justification and the other leads to sanctification. On the grounds of Christ's death for us, we are legally justified, but the indwelling Holy Spirit is designed to be experiential, flowing out of our lives, producing fruit, which is evidence of his presence and his working. Sometimes we are so taken up with Christ for us, the legality of our standing before God and our justification, but we don't always keep in parallel the indwelling of the Holy Spirit, designed to equip us to lead godly, fruitful lives.

The Spirit of wisdom and understanding

Secondly, in verse 2: 'The Spirit of the Lord will rest on him – the Spirit of wisdom and of understanding.' The first role of the Holy Spirit in our lives is that of revelation; he is the Spirit of wisdom, the Spirit of understanding. Paul wrote that someone without the Holy Spirit cannot accept or understand the things that come from the Spirit of God, because they are spiritually discerned (1 Corinthians 2:14). When he says they are 'spiritually discerned', he means it's not our intellect that gives us the capacity to hear God; it is that disposition of heart towards him as he reveals himself to us. Jesus prayed in Matthew 11:25–26, 'I praise you, Father, Lord of heaven and earth, because you have hidden these things from the wise and learned, and revealed them to little children. Yes, Father, for this was what you were pleased to do.' When he says, 'You have hidden these things from the wise and the learned', he is not being cruel to the clever; he's not being anti-intellectual or cynical about learning, as some evangelicals have been. He is simply saying that learning and education are not where you access God. 'He has revealed to little children' describes the disposition of our heart. It is the ears of our hearts that need to be open, and the Holy Spirit is the revealer.

Paul tells us in Romans 1 that God is revealing himself all the time to anyone who will tune their hearts to him. He reveals himself in creation, in conscience, by conviction as the Holy Spirit does that work of revealing. You know, it's always fun to discern where the Spirit of God is revealing Christ to people. One day, a young man telephoned me and asked if he could come and see me. He was a student at the University of Toronto, twenty-one years of age. He came into my study and said, 'I don't know what life is all about. I know it must have meaning. I've explored Islam and I am convinced it is not there. I have tried New Age philosophies and it's not there. I've read self-help books and it's like trying to pull yourself up with your shoelaces and it doesn't work. So I'd decided to have a look at Christianity and see if that makes sense. Last Sunday I came here to The Peoples Church. When I left, I hadn't understood a single word, but I knew it was true.'

The Holy Spirit bears witness to truth, and this poor guy was bearing witness to the truth before he knew what it was. The Holy Spirit was after him! We talked for a while, and I invited him to join a Bible study group that I have for young men who are either new Christians or not yet Christians. He joined that and we met once a month from about 6pm until 10 or 11pm. We would just sit around for the evening and talk about life and Scripture. After several months he came to Christ and he immediately began to witness and to disciple others. He ran his own little Bible study group for other students where he was staying, and I watched him grow very rapidly, recognizing the Holy Spirit had done the work that no human could do in revealing Christ to him. I then invited the young men in that group to come to my house at Christmas, and when they came he met my daughter. They got married two years ago, so he is now my son-in-law. A great godly young man from Iran, and how do you account for his conversion? It was the Holy Spirit of God revealing Christ.

The Trinity helps us in our evangelism. We are not on our own; we are not sales people; we are not trying to win an argument; we are working together with God. The words that we use may be clumsy, but at the same time the Holy Spirit is at work revealing. I would encourage you to keep your eyes open. Jesus said, 'Look out on the fields, they are ripe.' We don't always believe that. Ask God to open your eyes to what the Holy Spirit is doing and be caught up in the excitement of working together with him. This must have meant so much to Isaiah, because he had been told, as we mentioned yesterday, that he was to go and tell these people,

> Be ever hearing, but never understanding;
> be ever seeing, but never perceiving.
> (Isaiah 6:9)

But keep waiting, because the Spirit of God is going to do his work, as he always does.

The Spirit of counsel and power

Thirdly, the Spirit of the Lord is the Spirit of counsel and of power. You see, once the Holy Spirit has given us understanding, it is then the Spirit of counsel and of power that begins to work alongside us. This word 'counsellor' is used of the Holy Spirit in John 14 and 15. The more recent revised NIV has changed it to the word 'advocate', which is a good word. The word 'paraclete' is not easy to translate and doesn't have an exact English equivalent. But the Holy Spirit is often spoken of as being the counsellor in the sense that John records in his Gospel: 'He will be with you forever, he will teach and remind you of what I have told you and he will testify about me' (see John 14:26). So the Holy Spirit's ministry, as Jesus spoke of it there, is entirely centred upon Christ. I think that is an important thing for us to get hold of and to believe.

Have you ever noticed that the Holy Spirit has no personal name in the Bible? The Father does – Jehovah,

Immanuel, Elohim. The Son does – Jesus, which means Saviour; Immanuel, God with us; Christ. The Holy Spirit is given titles – the Counsellor, the Spirit of truth – but no personal name. Why? I suggest to you that it is because the Holy Spirit's task is not so much to make us conscious of the Holy Spirit, but to make us conscious of Christ. Jesus said that the Holy Spirit's task is to glorify me, to take the things that are mine and make them known to you. I get nervous when people just talk about the Spirit. There is something not quite right about that, because the Spirit's task is to make us conscious of Christ. Dr Campbell Morgan said from this platform that the evidence of the Holy Spirit's work is not so much that we are conscious of the Holy Spirit as that we are conscious of Christ. The Holy Spirit centres upon the work of Christ, and as he makes us more aware of Christ, the more we are living out of the richness of every spiritual blessing that we have in Christ, the more we are empowered to live godly and fruitful lives.

The Spirit of knowledge and the fear of the Lord

Then fourthly, in verses 2 and 3 Isaiah talks about the Spirit of knowledge and the fear of the Lord. It's interesting how the fear of God and knowledge are associated together in the Scriptures. For instance, Proverbs 1:7 says, 'The fear of the LORD is the beginning of knowledge.' Proverbs 9:10 says, 'The fear of the Lord is the beginning of wisdom, and knowledge of the Holy One is understanding.' Knowledge of God leads to a fear of God. And in case you worry that fear is a negative emotion, Isaiah adds, 'He will delight in the fear of the LORD' (verse 3).

The first time this phrase 'the fear of God' occurs is in Genesis 22, when God told Abraham to offer Isaac as a sacrifice at Mount Moriah. Abraham took Isaac on a three-day journey to the foot of the mountain. He left the servants behind and went up the mountain just with Isaac. Isaac was getting a little nervous, a little curious: 'We've got the wood, the fire, but where's the lamb?' 'God will supply the lamb. Don't ask any more questions, Isaac,' Abraham replied. And you remember how God told him to go and offer his son? Every promise God had ever made to Abraham was wrapped up in this son. Everything God had declared about Abraham, his legacy and his covenant with God, was dependent upon this son Isaac. Abraham made the altar and he bound his son. We don't know how old Isaac was, but there would have been some cooperation on Isaac's part. He must have trusted his father. Laying him on the altar, Abraham took the knife in his hand and was ready to thrust it into his son, believing, as the book of Hebrews tells us, that if necessary God would raise him from the dead, meaning that he was prepared to actually kill him. Suddenly God called from heaven, 'Do not do anything to him. Now I know that you fear God, because you have not withheld from me your son, your only son' (verse 12). 'Now I know,' said God, 'that you fear God' – that's the first time that phrase occurs in Scripture. What is this Spirit of the fear of God? It is sheer and total abandonment to God, obedience to him and trust in him, irrespective of the consequences.

The Holy Spirit brings us to the point where the Spirit of the fear of God is something we delight in. You will delight in the fear of the Lord, as the Lord Jesus did. We will say, 'Father, what happens to me in the process of doing your will is totally irrelevant to me as long as your will is done.' That was the prayer of Jesus in the garden of Gethsemane, wasn't it? 'If it is possible, may this cup be taken from me; if there is any other way that men and women, boys and girls, can be reconciled to a Holy God, nevertheless not as I will but as you will.' This time, of course, the Father did not intervene: the Son was crucified as our substitute. The work of the Spirit is not just to give us a good life, not just to help us along, not just to help us out of difficulties and problems, but to bring us to that point of complete abandonment to himself, irrespective of the consequences.

The Spirit working within us

Then in verse 5, Isaiah stops talking about the Spirit of the Lord resting on Jesus, the prototype of redeemed humanity, and therefore what it will mean for the Spirit of the Lord to rest on us. He now talks about what is going to be the consequence of the Holy Spirit's working within him. Verses 3–4 say,

> He will not judge by what he sees with his eyes,
> or decide what he hears with his ears;
> but with righteousness he will judge the needy.

His behaviour is going to be determined by this plumb line of righteousness, which is the character and holiness of God. Continuing in verse 4:

> With justice he will give decisions for the poor of the earth.
> He will strike the earth with the rod of his mouth;
> with the breath of his lips he will slay the wicked.
> Righteousness will be his belt
> and faithfulness the sash round his waist.

These verses say what is going to happen to this Branch: as the Holy Spirit works in him, he is going to be characterized by justice, faithfulness and righteousness.

You know, the work of the Holy Spirit in our lives is designed to make us effective in our world. He is not just here to bless me, but to make me a blessing: that is his purpose. In fact, Paul talks in Philippians 1:11 about 'being filled with the fruit of righteousness', and this is what he is describing here. The word 'fruit' is not in Isaiah 11, but it's a good description of what is described there. Galatians 5:22–23 talks about the fruit of the Holy Spirit: love, joy, peace, patience, kindness, goodness, faithfulness, gentleness and self-control. You may think it's a bit trivial, but I think it's very important: notice it is the *fruit* of the Spirit, not the *flowers* of the Spirit. You say, 'What's the difference?' Well, flowers are to make a place look nice; fruit has an entirely different function. What is fruit for? Fruit is for eating; it's not for decoration. You don't say, 'This place is a bit drab – hang up some bananas.' But you do say, 'I'm hungry – give me a banana.' The fruit of the Spirit is not so that you and I look good to other people. It's so that hungry people can feed on our love, patience, long-suffering and self-control, because it feeds their souls. And here in the life of Jesus, the Spirit of God will rest on him: the Spirit of wisdom and understanding, the Spirit of counsel and of power, the Spirit of knowledge and the fear of the Lord, and he'll delight in the fear of the Lord.

In a broken world, dirty women would talk to Jesus because they would feel comfortable with him. Lepers rang their bells saying, 'Unclean', and everybody crossed the road to avoid them, but Jesus always touched lepers every time he dealt with them. The disciples tried to keep the kids away, but Jesus said, 'Let them come to me.' And they clambered all over him. He loved them and they loved him, because the Spirit was in him. The Spirit in you and me is designed to express the faithfulness, righteousness and justice of Jesus. The work of the Spirit of God in the life of Jesus Christ and redeemed humanity will continue in our broken, fallen world, until one day when his righteousness, justice and faithfulness will be vindicated and the whole world will recognize who Jesus Christ is.

> The wolf will live with the lamb,
>   the leopard will lie down with the goat,
> the calf and the lion and the yearling together;
>   and a little child will lead them . . .
> for the earth will be filled with the knowledge of the LORD
>   as the waters cover the sea.
> (verses 6, 9)

That day is going to come in the future. In the meantime, we redeemed men and women are living in this fallen, broken world, indwelt by the Holy Spirit. The Spirit of God brings us to the point of living and delighting in the fear of God, so our neighbours know there is something different about us, because out of our lives flows fruit that feeds the deepest needs of their hearts. This is Isaiah's prophetic statement about what true redeemed humanity is going to be, and the prototype is the Lord Jesus himself. You and I are being conformed into the image of the Lord Jesus, and this is what he is making us to be.

Note

1. C. S. Lewis, *Mere Christianity* (William Collins, 2012).

4. Meeting the Deep Needs of the Heart: Isaiah 44 – 45

The sufficiency of God for his people

Water on the thirsty land

I want to build what I am going to share with you from chapters 44 and 45 around two very important promises. First in Isaiah 44:3, a promise is made to the people of God:

> For I will pour water on the thirsty land,
> and streams on the dry ground;
> I will pour out my Spirit on your offspring,
> and my blessing on your descendants.

Judah has been taken into exile by the Babylonians. Babylon had breathed down the neck of Judah for a number of years, and in three stages had invaded Judah and taken people away into exile, until the last stage when they besieged the city of Jerusalem for eighteen months. They starved the city into surrender and utterly destroyed it. So, when Nehemiah came back some years later, he could not take his mule through the city, because stones, rubble and destroyed buildings blocked everywhere. They took the people of God off into a Babylonian exile for seventy dark years. Less than fifty years after this, Babylon began to wane as the superpower of the Middle East, and Persia began to rise and in due course became the new master.

Isaiah is looking ahead to this period when the Persians are dominating the people of Israel in their exile, and he speaks words of hope. And if I can summarize, not just here, but some of the previous chapters too, Isaiah is saying that God chastises those he loves. This was not a calamity or an out-of-control event. Elsewhere in the Old Testament, God describes Nebuchadnezzar, the Babylonian king, as 'my servant' who has come for the purpose of disciplining and chastising. And the chastisement of God is not an end in itself; it's designed to correct and restore. When God brings chastisement and discipline to our lives, he is always remedial in his objectives that it might make us better people. Although if we do not respond to that chastisement, it will make us bitter people. Those are the options in our response to God's discipline: we become better or we become bitter.

God gives this promise of hope: 'I am going to satisfy the deep thirst of your souls and the deep thirst of the people of Israel.' The fulfilment of this was really at

Pentecost, when the Spirit was poured out. But what Isaiah 44:3 indicates is that there is a thirst in the souls of men and women that only God can satisfy. Every person has a thirst for something bigger than themselves and outside of themselves.

The deadly properties of idols

A big part of chapter 44 is given over to describing the alternatives by which we seek to satisfy our thirst, the alternatives to God himself. Isaiah talks about the futility of idol worship:

> All who make idols are nothing,
>   and the things they treasure are worthless.
> Those who would speak up for them are blind;
>   they are ignorant, to their own shame.
> (verse 9)

Look at the negative descriptions he gives of these people who've turned to idols: their treasure is worthless; they are blind and ignorant. Which begs the important question: 'Why in the world do people worship idols when they are worthless?' All over the world people engage in idol worship. The idolatry into which most people fall is not external idols of stone, but internal idols of the heart. John Calvin wrote that the human mind is a perpetual factory for idols, forever producing idols.

Tim Keller, in his excellent book *Counterfeit Gods*,[1] has come to the conclusion that most people today are being driven by a culture of idolatry. He describes idols as spiritual addiction to money, materialism, sex, power, body image, work, ambition, reputation and food. And this isn't new: Paul said that sexual immorality, impurity, lust, evil desires and greed are idolatry (Colossians 3:5). Keller defines an idol as something we cannot live without. He talks about money, which begins as a servant, becomes a powerful, life-altering, culture-shaping god that, as it grows in power, makes us do what we would not normally do, and eventually breaks the hearts of those who worship it. He talks about lust and sex as a driving power that, if you feed it enough, will become strong enough to break the rules intended to live by, and redefine what you see is right and wrong – it will master you. He talks about marriage when husbands lord it over their wives and wives manipulate and control their husbands; this ability to control becomes an idol. He talks about parents who plot out their children's lives and then resent it when their children naturally have their own ideas. He says these are all manifestations of idolatry, but our sense of significance, security and satisfaction is found in exercising this kind of power. Keller says that you know something is a god when you must have it, when you are driven to break the rules that you once honoured, when you are willing to harm others and even yourself in order to get it.

Now the message of Isaiah regarding idolatry is that, although it is empty in itself, it fills a need that was designed to be filled by God. When we become disconnected from the true God, we look for idols, because we can't live in a vacuum where nothing is driving us and giving our lives meaning. Something has to step into that vacuum. Nature abhors a vacuum; it will suck anything into it to fill it. If we deny the true God, we have to create an alternative god, and yet if we are rational about those gods, they are utterly futile. There is some brilliant sarcasm here in how Isaiah describes these gods. Let me read verse 12 to you:

> The blacksmith takes a tool
>   and works with it in the coals;
> he shapes an idol with hammers,
>   he forges it with the might of his arm.
> He gets hungry and loses his strength;
>   he drinks no water and grows faint.

In other words, building an idol doesn't energize him; it exhausts him. Isaiah talks about the carpenter in verses 13–17:

> The carpenter measures with a line
>   and makes an outline with a marker;
> he roughs it out with chisels
>   and marks it with compasses.
> He shapes it in human form,
>   human form in all his glory,
>   that it may dwell in a shrine.
> He cut down cedars,
>   or perhaps took a cypress or oak.

He let it grow among the trees of the forest,
  or planted a pine, and the rain made it grow.
It is used as fuel for burning;
  some of it he takes and warms himself,
  he kindles a fire and bakes bread.
But he also fashions a god and worships it;
  he makes an idol and bows down to it.
Half of the wood he burns in the fire;
  over it he prepares his meal,
  he roasts his meat and eats his fill.
He also warms himself and says,
  'Ah! I am warm; I see the fire.'
From the rest he makes a god, his idol;
  he bows down to it and worships.
He prays to it and says,
  'Save me! You are my god!'

How ridiculous! He cooks his food with the wood, warms himself with the wood and worships some of that same wood. Why does he behave so bizarrely? Because he has to. As Augustine famously said of God, 'You have made us for yourself and our hearts are restless until they find their rest in you.' We need to believe that about every human being we meet: we were made to know God and we fill ourselves with substitutes. G. K. Chesterton once said that any man who knocks on the door of a brothel is looking for God. Why? Because the search for intimacy and ecstasy, deep in his soul, was designed to be found in knowing and experiencing God. These men, says God to Isaiah, have set up idols in their hearts. People are asking the right questions, but they have no idea that the answer is God himself, and so instead the only alternative they have is idolatry.

And no-one has the discernment to see the emptiness of idolatry. Verses 19–20 say,

> No one stops to think,
> no one has the knowledge or understanding to say,
> 'Half of it I used for fuel;
> I even baked bread over its coals,
> I roasted meat and I ate.
> Shall I make a detestable thing from what is left?
> Shall I bow down to a block of wood?'
> Such a person feeds on ashes; a deluded heart misleads him;
> he cannot save himself, or say,
> 'Is not this thing in my right hand a lie?'

Of course it's a lie, but he does not have the knowledge or the discernment to recognize it, because in the human heart there is a God-shaped vacuum. It was Blaise Pascal who described it that way, and that vacuum sucks into it all kinds of idols.

The life-giving properties of the Holy Spirit

What is the remedy? The life-giving properties of the Holy Spirit. I'll read verse 3 again: 'I will pour water on the thirsty land, and streams on the dry ground.' The indication there is that the land, being a picture of the people, is thirsty.

I think it's a wonderful study to see how Jesus handled people. When he met the woman at the well in Samaria (John 4), you remember he offered her living water, the same image used here, and as he engaged her in conversation, he slowly unravelled her story. Remember, she had been married five times, and he asked her a very embarrassing question: 'Go, call your husband and come back.' She said, 'I don't have a husband.' And Jesus said, 'No, but you've had five and you are now living with a man to whom you are not married.' She had obviously been ostracized by the local people, and that's why she came alone in the heat of the day to the well. Of course she'd be ostracized – why wouldn't she be? She'd been married five times and she is now living with another man. Who's the next husband she's going to steal? You know, Jesus didn't criticize her for her failed marriages; he didn't criticize her sex life. He recognized that all of this was a symptom of a thirst and he said, 'Everyone who drinks this water will be thirsty again; this man you are now living with won't satisfy you because he cannot touch the deepest area of your heart.' But he said to her, 'Whoever drinks the water I give them will never thirst. Indeed, the water I give them will become in them a spring of water welling up to eternal life' (verse 14). Jesus is saying that if you drink what I am offering you, not only will this water satisfy your thirst; it will be in you like a well and a well is always deep, and it will be in you like a spring and a spring is always fresh – it will be a well of water springing up deep within you, producing something fresh every day.

And I ask you here this morning, 'What are you drinking to meet the deep needs of your soul?' We might say, 'We are at Keswick.' Therefore we assume we are drinking deeply from the Lord Jesus. But some of you have built an idol locked away deep inside your heart, and though you may be a Christian, that idol will increasingly push the Lord Jesus out of your life. You know, in Japan a lot of homes have a 'god shelf'. Often in Japan somebody says, 'Yes, I'd like to become a Christian', so they get some symbol of Christianity like a cross and they go home and they just move the gods along the god shelf to make room. Of course, that god shelf has to go if Christ is going to come. You know, we have god shelves in our hearts: those things tend to drive us and they tend to grow in power, and even though they are lifeless idols, they become controlling principles in our lives.

If you go back through the history of Israel, you realize that this whole exile was a chastisement because of their idolatry, and one of the things the exile did was to remove idolatry from Israel. You never again see, hear or read of Baals or Asherah poles. The exile cured them of idolatry, because sometimes God has to bring us to that point where we realize the utter bankruptcy of those idols and the bankruptcy of our own lives. After he has talked about the idols, Isaiah looks ahead to this period of captivity:

> Remember these things, O Jacob,
> for you are my servant, O Israel.

I have made you, you are my servant;
  O Israel, I will not forget you.
I have swept away your offences like a cloud,
  your sins like the morning mist.
Return to me,
  for I have redeemed you.
(verses 21–22)[2]

You see the passion of God here, as he speaks of 'O Jacob, O Israel'.

There is a passionate pleading here: 'O Israel, you have brought yourself into this place of bowing down to idols, but I have swept them away, and along with that sweeping away, I will pour out water on the thirsty land and streams on the dry ground.'

Getting rid of the idols isn't in itself the solution; replacing them with Jesus Christ and the Spirit of God is. That's why Jesus said that, if you cast a demon out of a man and don't replace it, the demon will come back seven times worse. That's why our ministry must always be positive: not just getting rid of idols, but coming to Jesus, finding in him that deep need of the heart being met and satisfied. You may have been a Christian for many years, as many of you have, but every day we need that fresh water in our own thirsty soul, that fresh receiving from Jesus, his presence, his life, his sufficiency for that deep need. After the exile, after the destruction of Jerusalem, Jeremiah walks through the rubble and writes the book of Lamentations. Lamentation means 'crying': it's just a book of tears, but in the midst of his tears he looks up and says,

> But this I call to mind,
> therefore I have hope:
> The steadfast love of the LORD never ceases;
> his mercies never come to an end;
> they are new every morning.
> (Lamentations 3:21–23)[3]

It's every morning: it's not living today on yesterday's supply, or living tomorrow on today's supply. You can't stockpile spiritual blessing in a week of Keswick to last you the next six months; you will need a fresh supply every day. The message of chapter 44 is the sufficiency of God for his people.

The sovereignty of God over his people

Treasures of darkness

In chapter 45 Isaiah turns his attention to Cyrus, the king of Persia, who has overrun the Babylonians and now has the fate of Israel in his hands. He is the most powerful man in the world. He says to them in verse 3,

> I will give you the treasures of darkness,
> riches stored in secret places,
> so that you may know that I am the LORD,
> the God of Israel, who summons you by name.

It's interesting to see what the Bible says about Cyrus. In Isaiah 44:28 God says of Cyrus,

> . . . He is my shepherd
> and will accomplish all that I please;
> he will say of Jerusalem, 'Let it be rebuilt,'
> and of the temple, 'Let its foundations be laid.'

And Cyrus was suddenly very kind to the occupied territories and peoples, and it was Cyrus who sent Ezra back to Jerusalem to rebuild the temple. What an amazing thing that God says of this pagan king: 'He is my shepherd' and 'This is what the LORD says to his anointed, to Cyrus, whose right hand I take hold of' (Isaiah 45:1). God is saying, 'You know, this is my anointed, and like a little boy I take him by the hand, even though he is the pagan king.' And in Isaiah 45:13 God promises, 'I will raise up Cyrus in my righteousness: I will make all his ways straight.'

What I want us to see from this is not only the sufficiency of God for his people in chapter 44, but the sovereignty of God over his people in chapter 45. God, in circumstances we often think are oppressive to us, is actually working to bring about his purpose, and he is bringing treasures out of darkness into our lives. Persia is today's Iran. Do you know, in the country of Iran there have been more converts to Christianity in the last twenty years than in the previous 2,000 years? In the Iranian diaspora, which is significant in many parts of the world, Iranians are coming to Christ. And do you know what triggered it? It was the 1979 revolution under Ayatollah Khomeini. As a result, the Iranian nation has become so disillusioned with Islam that many are turning to Christ. We can look at events through different eyes when we know that God is sovereign over the affairs of our world. We see the wonderful things that he is doing, even in places that we think are completely outside the will and purposes of God.

Egypt has been in the news a lot for the last two years since the 2011 revolution, and then of course again in May this year with the new revolution. But you know, God is doing amazing things in Egypt. The Cave Church in Cairo is affiliated with the Orthodox Church, but there is a wonderful movement of God in the Orthodox Church of Egypt. I met with the Minister of the Cave Church; it seats 10,000 people on the site of what was the garbage city of Cairo. They turned this big cave into a church and put seating in for 10,000 people, and they pack it out all the time. When I was in Cairo, they said, 'You know the good news? The Muslim Brotherhood, who are no longer in power, are creating agnosticism and atheism. People are becoming agnostic about Islam; they are becoming atheistic about Allah. They are not all coming to Christ, of course, but there are many who are, because they have been able to free themselves. They have become so disillusioned that they are turning to Christ.' 'I'll bring treasures out of darkness,' says the Lord.

Indonesia is the largest Muslim country in the world. I saw a video about six months ago produced by Muslims in Indonesia, warning that, if the Islamic community do not do something, Indonesia will be Christian by 2050. This was a Muslim film warning people to keep away from Christians, because people are coming to Christ! In a world that looks to be opposed to God, there are actually places where the darkness is producing treasure, as God promised Cyrus. In Argentina there has been a great revival. Do you know when it began? It began after the Falklands War. When the military junta, whom the people trusted, failed, and Britain rose up and humiliated them, the people became disillusioned, they lost their idol and they began to turn to God. I was in Chile not long ago. Do you know that in Chile they have a national day of evangelicals on 31 October? It commemorates the date that Martin Luther nailed his Thirty-Nine Articles to the church at Wittenberg. It is now a national holiday, and every church in Chile preaches the gospel on 31 October! Did you know there were so many Christians in Chile?

I am just sharing with you the principle that applies to the world we live in. God said to Cyrus, 'Cyrus, you are not part of the covenant people of God, but you are my shepherd. I take you by the right hand and I lead you and I am going to give treasures in the darkness; I am going to give riches which are stored in secret places.' If that is true of Cyrus' day, it is true globally about today. I know in our Western countries we are not seeing growth; we are seeing a marginalizing of the Christian faith, a reduction in numbers, by and large. Let's not panic. Maybe God is pushing us into a period of oppression. We may not be as free as we have been, and certainly not able to say the things we have been free to say from the Word of God. We may lose charitable status and all those kinds of things; we may be marginalized. But you know, it is in the darkness where God produces treasure. Let's trust him for that.

In our own lives, in the things that have gone so wrong, in the things that have hurt us so much, in the pain that we never anticipated, let's trust him. We gave our lives to God and then we ran into tragedy or somebody died who should never have died. Why in the world did God let this happen? Why did I get sick? Why did I lose my job? Here's the principle: 'I'll give you treasures in darkness, and I'll give you riches that are stored in secret places.' Why? So that you may know that I am God, so that you may say, 'This is not to do with anything I've done, nothing to do with my own manipulation or my own scheming; it's to do with God in his wonderful grace, love and sovereignty bringing about his purpose.' The Authorized Version gives a bad translation of Romans 8:28: 'All things work together for the good of those who love God.' 'Things' are passive, 'things' don't work, 'things' are not active. The better translation is the NIV: 'In all things God works for the good of those who love him, who have been called according to his purpose.' There are things that go wrong – the devil is the prince of this world, and there are things that are satanic going on all around us. But let's rest in the fact that 'In all things, whether good, bad or indifferent, God works for good.'

In chapter 44, Isaiah reminds us that we can know in our own hearts the sufficiency of God to meet our deepest need; otherwise, the vacuum in our hearts will express itself in idolatry. Chapter 45 is about the sovereignty of God in all the circumstances of our lives. We can trust and believe and know that one day out of the darkness will come treasure. Do you believe that?

Notes

1. Tim Keller, *Counterfeit Gods* (Hodder & Stoughton, 2010).
2. NIV 1984.
3. ESV.

5. The Suffering Substitute: Isaiah 53

Thank you for the privilege of being here this week and being able to open the Scriptures with you. I have known many of you for years. I didn't know I was so old, but some of you tell me that you knew me forty years ago! I tend to forget that so many years have passed by. It's been wonderful to meet new people as well, and to sense the appetite here in this tent for the Word of God.

In choosing which chapters to look at in the book of Isaiah, I have borne in mind the theme of the transforming Trinity. We have looked at chapters that are devoted to the Holy Spirit (Isaiah 11), Isaiah's vision of God in chapter 6, and I suppose no chapter focuses more clearly on the work of the Son than Isaiah 53. You know, most people on the street have a simple creed, and it goes like this: God punishes bad people and rewards good people. The Bible disagrees, and in Romans 4:5 Paul makes a very remarkable statement, where he speaks of God who justifies the wicked. Now that throws a curve ball at the whole moral order of the universe. It offends our instinct for justice. But I want to show you from Isaiah 53 the basis on which God justifies the wicked, because this is the tremendous ground on which you and I as Christians stand: we do not receive what our sins deserve.

This portrait of the suffering servant in Isaiah 53 would have come as a shock to the Israelites to whom Isaiah gave this. Their vision of the Messiah was as a triumphant king. That vision does come through the book of Isaiah as well, but we've got this other story which is the story of a servant. Not only a suffering servant, but a suffering substitute, who stands before God on behalf of sinful people. This chapter is full of the language of substitution. Let me give you just seven couplets: 'Surely he [Christ] took up our infirmities and carried our sorrows' (verse 4); 'he was pierced for our transgressions' (verse 5); 'he was crushed for our iniquities' (also in verse 5); later in that same verse, 'the punishment that brought us peace was on him, and by his wounds we are healed'; 'the LORD has laid on him the iniquity of us all' (verse 6); 'he bore the sin of many, and makes intercession for the transgressors' (verse 12). You've got seven couplets here which look ahead to Christ as our substitute and the benefits we have because of him. No wonder Isaiah's opening statement is: 'Who has believed our message?' The idea was unbelievable to the Jewish people who first read this, and still is to the Jewish people today. They see this as a description of how the nation of Israel had suffered through the years, but they cannot explain the substitutionary nature of that.

The Father was satisfied

I want to look at three themes in this chapter regarding this suffering, substituting servant. First, let's talk about the Father being satisfied. If I were to ask you for whom did Jesus die, I wonder how you might answer? You might answer, 'Jesus died for the world', or you may say, 'Jesus died for sinners', or you may personalize it and say, 'Jesus died for me.' All those statements of course contain truth, because we are the beneficiaries of his death, but we are not the prime reasons why Jesus died and why the cross was necessary. In the first instance, Jesus died for his Father; he died for God. Let me show you some statements here: 'we considered him stricken, smitten by God' (verse 4); 'the LORD [that is God] has laid on him the iniquity of us all' (verse 6); 'it was the LORD's will to crush him . . . the LORD makes his life an offering for sin' (verse 10). It is the Father who requires the cross. We would prefer a much simpler, more straightforward remedy for our sin. Our preferred remedy would be: as long as you are really sorry, as long as you truly repent, God will forgive you. Wouldn't that be enough? But it isn't. You see, if the solution to sin was that as long as you repent you will be forgiven, you don't need the cross.

Sin in the first instance is not portrayed as a problem to us; it is portrayed as a problem to God: it has violated his righteousness and provoked his wrath. That is the essential problem with sin. If the problem with sin was that it messes up our lives, the solution is very straightforward: be forgiven, stop doing it, get some counselling if that will help you, and straighten up your life. But that doesn't begin to deal with sin, because the issue is not that it messes us up, though it does; the real issue with sin is that it provokes the wrath of God. Now in the book of Isaiah, the word 'wrath' appears in relation to God and his disposition to sin twenty times, and another twenty times Isaiah speaks of God's anger. So forty times he speaks of his anger and wrath. We can't look at all of them, but let me take you back to Isaiah 51:17:

> Awake, awake!
> Rise up, O Jerusalem,
> you who have drunk from the hand of
> the LORD
> the cup of his wrath,
> you who have drained to its dregs
> the goblet that makes people stagger.

He talks there about the cup of his wrath in verse 20: 'They are filled with the wrath of the LORD, with the rebuke of your God.' Now that is our problem: our sin provokes the wrath and the anger of God. If you go on a bit later to Isaiah 63:6:

I trampled the nations in my anger;
in my wrath I made them drunk
and poured their blood on the ground.

Now here is God talking about his anger, talking about his wrath and about shedding blood. Then in the next verse, it seems almost schizophrenic, because he says,

I will tell of the kindnesses of the LORD,
the deeds for which he is to be praised,
according to all the LORD has done for us –
yes, the many good things
he has done for Israel.

Isaiah talks about the anger of God, the wrath of God, the shedding of blood, and in verse 7 the kindness of God, the compassion of God and the good things that we may receive from God. Now how does the anger and wrath of God turn to compassion and kindness? This change of standing is only possible because of Isaiah chapter 53.

Now I want to explain to you that what lies behind the cross is not in the first instance the love of God. Of course, God is love as his very nature, but what lies behind the cross is the wrath of God. The brutality of the cross is an expression of God's anger. There is an important word, 'propitiation'. It's in the King James Version, but has got lost in a lot of translations. It's back in the English Standard Version, and I am going to quote the following verses from that translation. The word 'propitiate' means to turn away wrath by satisfying its demands and its requirements. So Romans 3:24–25 says that we are, 'justified by his grace as a gift, through the redemption that is in Christ Jesus, whom God put forward as a propitiation by his blood, to be received by faith'. What he is saying is that God has put Jesus Christ forward to address and satisfy the wrath of God. 1 John 2:2 says, 'He is the propitiation for our sins, and not for ours only but also for the sins of the whole world.' 1 John 4:10 says, 'In this is love, not that we have loved God but that he loved us and sent his Son to be the propitiation for our sins.' Now this idea of propitiation has been controversial and still is. We do not like the idea that God's anger needs to be addressed; it does not fit the stereotype we have created of him. But that is not true to the record of Scripture. It is God the Father who strikes out at the Son. Not just stricken by evil men, though he was, but stricken by God, smitten by him. Verses 6 and 10 say, 'the Lord has laid on him the iniquity of us all . . . Yet it was the Lord's will to crush him . . . the Lord makes his life an offering for sin.' This is the wrath of God being poured out on his Son as our substitute, standing in the place that our sin created.

If we think of sin as our problem because it messes us up and gets us into trouble, and we do not think of sin first and foremost as a problem to God which provokes his wrath and anger, we probably sentimentalize the cross, and our tears of repentance will be in danger of being little more than tears of self-pity. There are two things in the character of God that make the cross necessary: his justice on the one hand and his mercy on the other.

Now you all know that God is just and you all know that God is merciful, but when you think about those two attributes in the character of God, you realize that they are actually incompatible with each other. Justice is giving people what they deserve, and mercy is not giving people what they deserve. How are justice and mercy reconciled? Supposing I was in court for some crime and I was found guilty. The magistrate could act justly and punish me by fining me £1,000. Or he could be merciful to me and let me go free. What he can't do is both! But he is obligated to be just because that is his job as a magistrate, and so he fines me £1,000. And supposing my friend Peter Maiden takes out his cheque book and he writes a cheque for £1,000, goes to the clerk of the court and says, 'Here is a cheque for £1,000 to cover the fine of Charles Price.' The record of that court would say, 'Charles Price: guilty. Punishment: paid'. And as far as the court is concerned, justice has been done, but as far as I am concerned personally, mercy has been received only because a third party has stepped into the situation and paid my fine in full. It's not a complete illustration, but it helps us. The wages of sin is death; the wrath of God has been provoked to the extent that the just response to our sin is that we die. But Jesus, the third party, steps into the situation. He satisfies and absorbs the justice of God, so that we might go free as the recipients of his mercy.

Now having said that, I want to ask you a very important question: when you appeal to God for forgiveness, do you appeal to his justice or to his mercy? The answer is we appeal to his justice. 1 John 1:9 says, 'If we confess our sins, he is faithful and just.' God forgives you on the basis of his justice. Go back to the illustration: as I begin to walk out of the court, someone stops me and says, 'Aren't you the guy who was fined £1,000? Where are you going?' 'I'm going home.' On what basis? £1,000 has been paid, and on the grounds of justice I can walk out of that court room. That's why the Bible talks about us being justified, not about being mercified!

The sinner is justified

Now that leads me to my second point: that the sinner is justified. In verse 11, Isaiah writes,

> After the suffering of his soul,
>   he will see the light of life and be satisfied;
> by his knowledge my righteous servant will justify many,
>   and he will bear their iniquities.

You are familiar with the word 'justified' because it is part of the Christian vocabulary. It is a legal term and it means justice has been satisfied. To be justified is not another word for being forgiven; it has an entirely different meaning. To be justified means that the case is over.

Let me give you an illustration of this. When Britain had capital punishment, if a man was hanged in Scotland, a notice was posted outside the prison announcing the hanging. It had certain required legal language and it would say, 'On such-and-such a date, at Market Cross, so-and-so (naming the prisoner) was justified.' What did it mean? Did it mean he had been forgiven? No, it meant justice had been satisfied: the case is over, the judge has taken off his wig and gone home, the policemen have been assigned to another case and the lawyers are on to another job. It's over and that crime can never again be resurrected in a court of law, because to be justified means that it is over. Justified is not just about being forgiven; it is much deeper than that. It means that the case is over, it is finished.

Now of course it is true that the mercy of God and the love of God lie behind the cross, but if God were to forgive us on the basis of mercy alone, we might be forgiven, but we would not be justified. We are justified on the grounds that Jesus Christ satisfied the justice of God, and it is over. Now those of you who appeal to God's mercy – at some time in your Christian life, you'll confess to God the sin you confessed the previous day and so many times before, and you'll wonder if you've not exhausted his mercy. But when you appeal to his justice, God is legally and morally obligated to forgive. He is faithful and just and he forgives.

Supposing on Monday morning this week you arrived here and you needed a cup of coffee. You went into the café and said, 'I'd love a cup of coffee, but I forgot to bring any money with me this morning. Would you mind just giving me a cup of coffee?'

The person behind the counter says, 'Well, I'm not supposed to do this, but all right. Don't tell anybody, enjoy your coffee.' On Tuesday morning you arrive here before the meeting, go to the café and say, 'Good morning, I'd love a cup of coffee this morning, but you'd never believe it, I forgot my money again.' 'Listen chum, we gave you a cup of coffee yesterday. We are not supposed to just give away coffee.' 'Well, did anyone know? Did you get into trouble? Go on, just give me a cup of coffee, please.' Meanwhile, the line of people behind you is getting longer, so they say, 'OK, don't do it again. Here's your coffee.' But supposing I knew you and knew that you didn't carry any money, and I went into the café on Monday morning and said, 'There's a friend of mine coming up to the Bible readings and he never carries any money, but he loves a cup of coffee. Here's £10 to get him some coffee.' So you arrive on Monday morning and go up to the counter and say, 'I'd love a cup of coffee, but I've forgotten to bring any money. Can you give me a cup of coffee?' 'What's your name? Oh sure, here's a cup of coffee.' You go back again on Tuesday and say, 'I don't have any money.' 'No problem, here's a cup of coffee. Would you like a latte?' What's the difference? There's cash in the till. The first time you are appealing to mercy, and they may or may not give it to you. But now they are obligated to give you the coffee because I gave them £10.

I don't want to trivialize the grounds of our forgiveness, but the point is: there is cash in the till! When you and I come in repentance and say, 'Lord Jesus, I have failed again. Father, would you forgive me?' He looks to the cross and sin is paid for. We have no cash of our own – Romans 5:6 says, 'When we were still powerless, Christ died for us';

Romans 5:8: 'While we were still sinners, Christ died for us'; Romans 5:10: 'When we were God's enemies, we were reconciled to him through the death of his Son.' We have nothing but Jesus. Christ has satisfied the just demands of God, and although God is merciful, we appeal to his justice, which is why we are justified.

I have little doubt that there are lots of folk here this morning and there are sins from your past that rise up and condemn you because you have not understood you are justified. On the grounds of justice, the case against you is over because Christ absorbed the justice of God. Archbishop William Temple, Archbishop of Canterbury early in the twentieth century, explained that the only contribution we make to our salvation is the sin that makes it necessary for us to be saved. Otherwise, it is the love of God expressed in the cross of Christ that satisfies the justice of God.

Our sin is buried

A neglected area in our thinking is that our sin is buried. Isaiah 53:9 says,

> He was assigned a grave with the wicked,
> and with the rich in his death.

Now we do not make much of the burial of Jesus in our Christian teaching, but it is important. Historically, Jesus should not have been buried, because in Jerusalem the bodies of criminals were thrown into a deep narrow gorge on the south side of the city of Jerusalem, which is known as the Valley of Gehenna. In Jesus' day, it was known as the garbage dump of Jerusalem, and you threw everything down into this valley where a fire burned continually so it all burnt up. But Jesus was not placed there, because Joseph of Arimathea, a member of the Sanhedrin, approached Pilot to ask for the body of Jesus (John 19:38). And with Pilot's permission, Joseph took Jesus away, and this remarkable prophecy in Isaiah 53:9 was fulfilled:

> He was assigned a grave with the wicked,
> and with the rich man in his death.

Now this is significant, because there is a finality to burial.

The burial of Jesus is an important part of our doctrine of the crucifixion. At Calvary he bore our sin, he satisfied the wrath of God and he legally removed our guilt so that we are justified. And having died, he was buried. And not only have we died with Christ; we are buried with him too (Romans 6:4). Isaiah 53:9 says, 'He was assigned a grave with the wicked', and he is talking about what is happening to our sin. There is an old hymn that many of you will know. It summarizes the whole work of Jesus:

> Living, He loved me; dying, He saved me;
> Buried, He carried my sins far away;
> Rising, He justified freely forever:
> One day He's coming – O glorious day![1]

But don't skip over that second line: 'Buried, He carried my sins far away.'

If we don't have a clear doctrine of being buried with Christ, it is quite likely our sins will continue to haunt us. Romans 8:1 says, 'Therefore, there is now no condemnation for those who are in Christ Jesus.' But you don't know how many times I've sat with somebody who has been a Christian many years but is living under a sense of condemnation. Partly that's because they don't understand that they were justified legally, and partly because they don't understand that our sin was buried – it's past tense. You know, whenever we feel condemned, you can be sure it's not God speaking. It's the devil speaking about our sin. He is the accuser of our brothers who accuses us before God day and night (Revelation 12:10). There are two people who speak to us about our sins: the devil and the Holy Spirit. The devil condemns and the Holy Spirit convicts. Here's the difference: condemnation is like a wet blanket that sits on you and you can't get out of it; conviction makes us aware of our sin, but at the same time the Holy Spirit points us to the cross and offers us cleansing forgiveness.

Maybe there are those of us here this morning who are plagued with a sense of guilt. Listen to verse 12:

> [He] was numbered with the transgressors.
> For he bore the sin of many,
> and made intercession for the transgressors.

'He was numbered with the transgressors' means he was

identified as one of us. He became a sinner in his standing before the Father: he who knew no sin was made to be sin for us. 'He was numbered with the transgressors so that he might make intercession for the transgressors.' What does that mean? It means that he stands between the transgressor and God; he stands on our behalf facing the Father, speaking on our behalf as our advocate. So he says to the Father, 'Charles Price has done it again: he has confessed; he's come clean about it.' The sin leaves our body through our mouth, and Jesus says, 'Father, I am speaking from his side, I'm on his side, I am his defender, I am his advocate. On the grounds of my own death, he is forgiven; he's justified.' Isn't that fantastic? This is the language of substitution: Christ was made sin – that means he stood in my place, so in reverse I am made righteous and I stand in his place. Substitution works both ways: he was made sin in my place and I am made righteous in his place.

God once looked at Jesus Christ and saw me in all my sin. Now God looks at me and he sees Jesus in all his righteousness. That's substitution both ways – his sin was not about him, it was about me; and my righteousness is not about me, it's about him. That righteousness is an imputed one that comes from the Lord Jesus Christ. It's not being humble to doubt your forgiveness, because doubts about your forgiveness are doubts about Jesus. Of course, we don't deserve forgiveness, but when we doubt that we are clean before God, we doubt the effectiveness of the cross. Here's a beautiful verse, 1 John 4:17: 'In this way, love is made complete among us so that we will have confidence on the day of judgment.' We are going to stand before God with confidence – not self-confidence, not pride, not arrogance – but in utter humility, confident that Jesus Christ is enough.

So, I finish with verses 4 and 5:

> Surely he took up our infirmities
>   and carried our sorrows,
> yet we considered him stricken by God,
>   smitten by him, and afflicted.
> But he was pierced for our transgressions,
>   he was crushed for our iniquities;
> the punishment that brought us peace was upon him,
>   and by his wounds we are healed.

What was imposed upon Jesus was our infirmities, our sorrows, our transgressions, our iniquities and our punishment. What was imposed upon us is peace and healing. Do you actually believe that? If you don't, you'll be considering that your cleanliness and your godliness have something to do with how well you perform. But it has everything to do with what Jesus Christ did. Although we don't deserve it, we can say, 'Thank you, Lord. I am justified. The hanging is over, the case is closed, the judge is off his bench, the policemen are doing something else and the lawyers are out of a job. It's over. I am justified and my sin in the person of Jesus Christ is buried. It's over. It's over.'

* All quotes from NIV 1984, unless otherwise stated.

Note

1. J. Wilbur Chapman, 'One Day'.

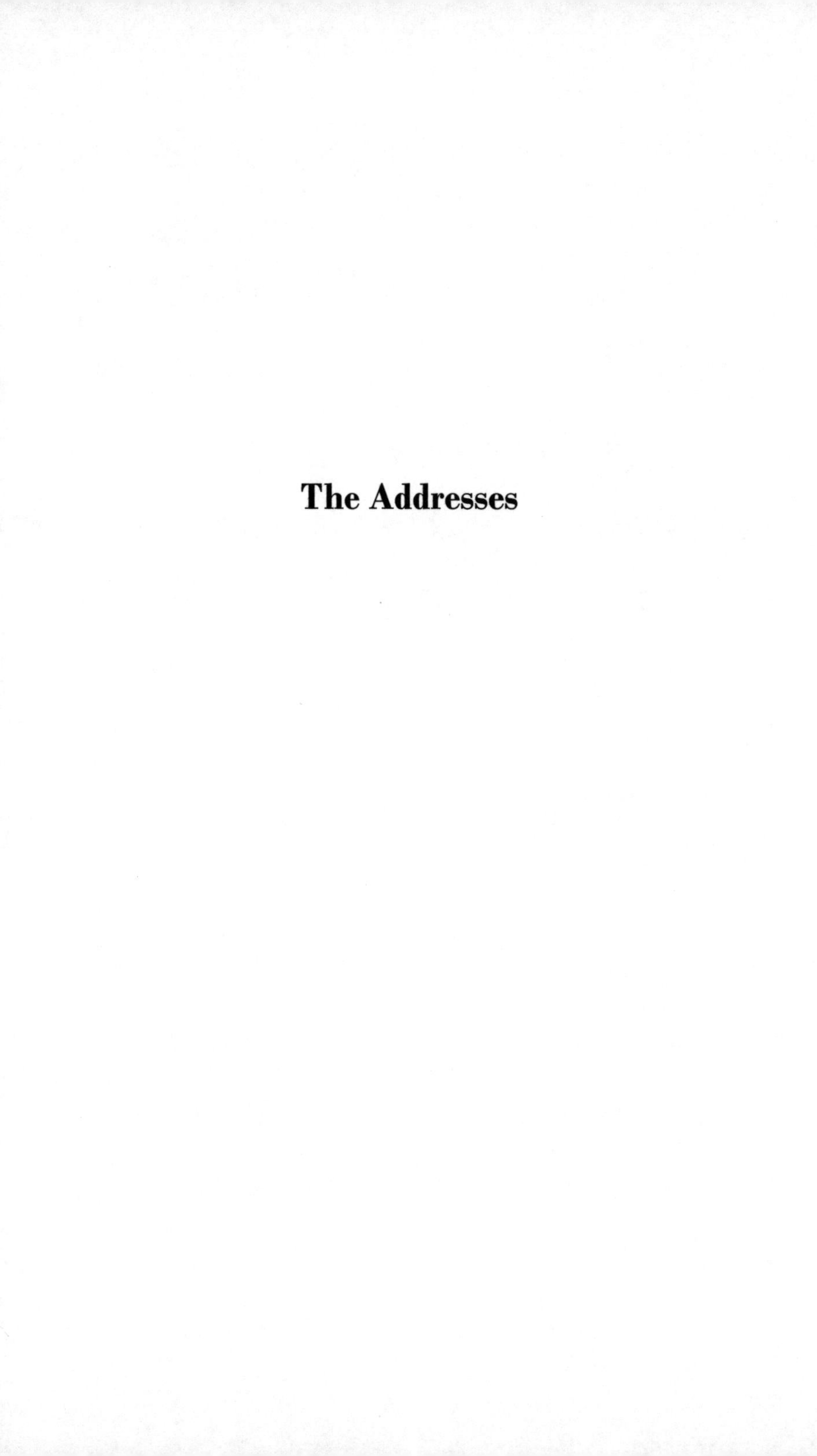

The Addresses

Saved by the Triune God

by John Risbridger

John Risbridger has been at Above Bar Church in Southampton since September 2004, serving as Minister and Team Leader. He worked for five years in hospital management before joining UCCF in 1994, working first as a Regional Team Leader and then as Head of Student Ministries. John is Chairman of Keswick Ministries. He is married to Alison and they have two daughters.

Saved by the Triune God: Mark 1:1–20

How did you feel when Andy Murray lifted the Wimbledon trophy a few weeks ago, or when Chris Froome stood on the middle podium and lifted the cup for the Tour de France? At the end of the Wimbledon final, our household erupted with screams of delight. It was good news! After seventy-seven years, a Wimbledon champion! We like good news: it lifts our spirits, renews our hope and energizes our lives. Our passage this evening is about good news.

Mark 1:1 reads: 'The beginning of the good news about Jesus the Messiah, the Son of God'. This is the title and contents page of the book we call 'Mark's Gospel' – probably the earliest account we have of Jesus' life, based on the testimony of those who saw him. The coming of Jesus is good news which lifts our spirits, renews our hope and transforms our lives.

Our focus at Keswick this week is on the transforming Trinity, and that transforming work begins right here with the gospel itself. The gospel is about the *Son* (Jesus Christ, verse 1), who was sent in accordance with the *Father's* purpose (verses 2–3), in order to baptize us with the *Holy Spirit* (verses 4–8). And as the *Son comes* into the public sphere of human history at his baptism (verse 9), the *Spirit descends on him* (verse 10) and the *Father speaks over him*: 'You are my Son, whom I love; with you I am well pleased' (verse 11). The Holy Trinity is conspiring together for us and for our salvation, which is why this evening we can joyfully celebrate the security of our salvation and the sufficiency of the gospel, because it rests not on ourselves, but on the Father's steadfast purpose, the Son's perfect obedience and the Spirit's life-giving power.

But the gospel isn't just a philosophy of life; it is about a *person*. It's about someone who lived in history: Jesus of Nazareth who is the Messiah, Christ, God's promised King and rescuer, the Son of God. The rest of the book sets out why Mark, and many others, became convinced that this is really true. If you're not sure that it's true, we're delighted that you're here this evening. But why not read Mark's Gospel through and assess the evidence for yourself? Christian faith isn't meant to be blind faith. The Bible doesn't just shout at us and tell us we must believe; it helps us see why. So let's begin by looking at one of the many lines of evidence.

The witnesses (verses 2–13)

There are three witnesses to Jesus here, and each highlights something of who he is and why he has come.

The witness of Old Testament Scripture: he is God coming to rescue us (verses 2–3)

Imagine you go home tonight and hear a knock on your door. A smartly dressed lady is there with a fine English accent. 'I'm the Queen,' she announces. You wouldn't believe it, would you, because Her Majesty doesn't turn up unannounced. Similarly, Jesus didn't just turn up unannounced; his coming had been promised for centuries.

In verses 2–3, Isaiah, who wrote over 700 years before Jesus came, said God would send a messenger: a voice who would call out in the wilderness telling people they must prepare for the Lord, that is God, because he was coming to rescue them. They must make a straight path for him to enter their lives. We'll see in a moment whose voice that was. But for now, notice that Isaiah said the voice would call people to prepare for the coming of God himself, God coming to rescue them.

The witness of John the Baptist: he is powerful and will baptize us with the Holy Spirit (verses 4–8)

Verse 4 reads: 'And *so* John the Baptist appeared in the wilderness.' In other words, our second witness is the fulfilment of what the first witness had promised. He is 'the voice' who called in the wilderness. He was clearly not your regular kind of guy. 'John wore clothing made of camel's hair, with a leather belt around his waist, and he ate locusts and wild honey' (verse 6). That probably meant he had low cholesterol and plenty of protein! Did you hear that the UN Food and Agricultural Organization recently told us that we should eat more insects like locusts, because they are high in fibre and protein, and low in saturated fat? But that's not quite the point! What Mark is saying is that John is the last in a long line of Old Testament prophets who were all looking forward to the coming of God. Elijah, the most famous prophet, had a lifestyle much like John's (see 2 Kings 1:8).

John's message is that all this expectation is about to be fulfilled because Jesus is coming. So people must get ready. How? How can we make a straight path for God into our lives? Verse 4 explains that John came, 'preaching a baptism of repentance for the forgiveness of sins'. That word 'repentance' is about changing our minds about ourselves and about God. It's about stopping comparing ourselves with one another and thinking we're OK, and starting to compare ourselves with God and realizing that we're not OK and we need his forgiveness. It's about stopping running *from* God and pushing him out of our lives, and turning round to run *towards* him and welcoming him in.

That's what John's baptism symbolized. As people came to him to be plunged under the water, they were saying they wanted their sins forgiven, and their old life, lived as if God wasn't there, washed away. And today, the way to make a straight path into your life for God is still the same – whether for the first time or the five hundredth. It's about seeking God's forgiveness and turning round, so we're no longer pushing God away but welcoming him. So let me ask you, is there a straight path for God into your life at the beginning of this Keswick week? Is your heart like a clenched fist, closed off to God and resistant to the challenges and invitations of his Word, as if they are all for someone else? Or is your heart tender towards him, quick in repentance, hungry to meet him?

But what was Jesus coming for? John explained, 'After me comes the one more powerful than I, the straps of whose sandals I am not worthy to stoop down and untie' (verse 7). Sorting out sandals and feet was a slave's job, but John knew that 'the one coming is so great and powerful that I'm not even worthy to be his slave'. And when he comes he will 'baptise you with the Holy Spirit' (verse 8). The Holy Spirit is the living presence of God, so John is saying that when Jesus comes he will plunge us not into water, but into the living, transformational active presence of God in our lives. That is the good news! That's what Jesus came to do. He didn't come to start a new religion, but to save a people who would know their God and live in relationship with him.

A couple of weeks ago I sat in a small group in our church prayer meeting. Beside me was a young woman who had come to faith a couple of months ago. What a joy to hear her pray – no layers of theological jargon, no façade of religious pretence – just a young woman pouring out her heart to the God she had come to know in Jesus Christ and by the Holy Spirit. That's what Jesus came to do!

The witness of God the Father: he is God's Son, who fulfils the Father's plan in the Spirit's power (verses 9–13)

So Jesus comes to be baptized by John, and as he comes up from the water, it becomes clear that what John has been saying is true. Jewish people spoke of the 'closing of heaven' as a way of saying that God's blessing had been withdrawn, but now in verse 10 heaven is torn open for the blessing of the Holy Spirit to descend. He descends on Jesus as the Spirit of love, revealing the Father's love for him (as later he will do for us, Romans 5). And he descends on him as the Spirit of power, so that he is able, as John said, to plunge us into the life of the Holy Spirit.

So we hear the words of the third witness, who is God the Father: 'You are my Son, whom I love; with you I am well pleased' (verse 11). Who is Jesus? He is the eternally loved Son of God, who has for all eternity been his joy and delight. What an insight into the nature of God – even before he is the Sovereign Creator, God is the eternal God and Father of our Lord Jesus Christ who has always been bringing forth his Son and, in the union of the Holy Spirit, always delighting in the Son he has brought forth. He is that kind of God. And since he is that kind of God, we can say that everlasting joy and overflowing love lie at the heart of the universe. What an insight into the sublime majesty and beauty of Jesus. Imagine the infinite capacity of the heart of God. What could possibly satisfy that infinite heart for all eternity? The answer is: 'Jesus', whose glory and beauty are such that he has filled the Father's heart for all eternity with infinite and everlasting joy!

But Jesus also pleases the Father because he perfectly fulfils the Father's plan, and he does so in the face of opposition and suffering. You can see some of that opposition in verses 12–13. But what is the plan? You need to read the rest of Mark's Gospel to find the answer, but there is a hint of it here. Remember why John was baptizing people? Verse 4 says, 'John the Baptist appeared in the wilderness, preaching a baptism of repentance for the forgiveness of sins.' And do you remember what the Father said of Jesus in verse 11? 'You are my Son, whom I love; with you I am well pleased.' So why was Jesus sharing in a baptism that symbolized repentance and the forgiveness of sins when he had no sins of his own? The answer can only be that he had come to identity himself with sinful people like me and you; to stand where we stand, in our place.

That identification with us would go on to reach its climax when he died, hanging on a cross for us. He even called his death a baptism (Mark 10:38–39), indicating that it completed what was begun here in his baptism by John. He died on the cross not for his own sins – because the Father was well pleased with him – but for our sins. He stood in our place, he took what we deserved, he died the death that we deserved for our rebellion against God, and he did it so we don't have to, so that we can be forgiven and brought back to God.

And that completes the picture. Who is Jesus? Listen to the witnesses! He is God coming among us; he is the powerful One – the promised Saviour, the Messiah; he is the perfect Son of God. What did he come to do? Listen to the witnesses! The Son came to fulfil the Father's rescue plan, dying on the cross for us, so that we could be forgiven and brought into this wonderful new relationship with God by the Holy Spirit – a transforming relationship with the transforming Trinity that continues beyond death into everlasting life! That's the good news!

So, those were the witnesses who help us understand who Jesus was and why he came. Now, very briefly:

The message (verses 14–15)

'After John was put in prison, Jesus went into Galilee, proclaiming the good news of God. "The time has come," he said. "The kingdom of God has come near. Repent and believe the good news!"' (Mark 1:14–15). In other words, all the decades of waiting are over. Just as Isaiah had said, in the coming of Jesus, God is stepping into human history and beginning to reign. He is coming to put things right. He is coming to rescue us. He is coming to bring us back to God. It's good news!

Let's imagine you get an email tonight with some good news. A friend has arranged a two-week holiday for you on a perfect tropical island – all expenses paid! One phone call is all it will take to arrange the date and then it's yours. How will you respond to the good news? Sit on it? No, you'll be on the phone at the first opportunity!

So, what about our response to the good news about Jesus? We face a choice. We can continue to live as if Jesus hadn't come, as if we didn't need forgiveness, as if we weren't made for him. Or we can turn around – we can repent, stop running away and turn from life with us at the centre, and believe the good news. Believe that we can know God through his Son Jesus. But this believing isn't just something in our brains, like I believe Keswick is in the Lake District. It's relational; it's belief in the sense of personal, active trust. Trust that Jesus came for *you*; trust him to forgive *your* sins through his death on the cross; trust him to baptize *you* with his Holy Spirit and bring *you* into this new relationship with God. But it doesn't stop there:

The invitation (verses 16–20)

'As Jesus walked beside the Sea of Galilee, he saw Simon and his brother Andrew casting a net into the lake, for they were fishermen. "Come, follow me," Jesus said, "and I will send you out to fish for people." At once they left their nets and followed him' (Mark 1:16–18). Jesus gives an invitation to an ongoing relationship: 'Come, follow me.' He is not talking about adding a nice little bit of religion onto an otherwise nearly perfect life, like a dusting of icing sugar on top of a wonderful sponge cake. No! This invitation is much more radical and much more exciting than that. It's an invitation to join the greatest adventure on earth, as we follow Jesus in changing the world, through his life-transforming message of good news! He invites us to fish for people: that means telling our friends, our neighbours, our colleagues the good news that there is a God in heaven – the Father who loves us, the Son who came for us, the Spirit who gives us life – and that this God, the transforming Trinity, calls us to know him.

That's the invitation Jesus is making in this passage, and it's an invitation to us all.

Have you listened to the witnesses?

Have you believed the message?

Have you accepted the invitation and begun the great adventure of passing on the good news to others?

Knowing the Father

by Paul Williams

Paul Williams is the Vicar of Christ Church Fulwood in Sheffield. Before training for the ordained ministry, he worked in a bank and then the newspaper industry. He is married to Caroline and they have three children: Susannah, Bethan and Joshua.

Knowing the Father: 1 John 2:28 – 3:10

In his book *Run Baby Run*,[1] Nicky Cruz describes how he was saved by Christ out of a life of crime as a gang warlord in New York City. He was raised in a terrible neighbourhood in Puerto Rico by parents who were spiritists. His parents mentally abused him, his own mother repeatedly calling him 'son of Satan'. When he was fifteen years old, his parents sent him to live with his older brother in New York City. There he ran away and started living on the streets and became a member of a gang. To cut a long story short, he met the preacher David Wilkerson, who told him that God loved him. At that first meeting he threatened to kill the preacher, but it wasn't long before he asked God for forgiveness and started to follow Jesus Christ.

It's a most wonderful story of a life completely transformed by the grace of Jesus Christ. But I mention Nicky

Cruz this evening because there was another remarkable change that came about in his life. Fred Sanders writes of Nicky Cruz, 'First he saw the Trinity as a difficult doctrine that had to be accepted but could hardly be explained, then he went on to see it as an illuminating doctrine that explained what he read in the Bible and what he experienced in his actual Christian life. Whereas he first encountered the doctrine [of the Trinity] as a problem, he came to understand it as a solution.'[2]

And Sanders suggests that's true for many Christians. 'We tend to acknowledge the doctrine [of the Trinity] with a polite hospitality but not welcome it with any special warmth.'[3] But as we consider the nature of God in the Trinity, and tonight as we think about the love of the Father, it should be life-transforming. A right understanding of our God should change the way we live. And so, as we look at this passage in 1 John, I want to think about it with the doctrine of the Trinity in mind, seeing how it helps us understand the Trinity and how understanding the Trinity leads us to live out the implications of this passage.

God is love

As we read of the love of the Father, we can easily let it pass us by without really thinking about it. We're so familiar with it. We know that God is love. Indeed, it is John who writes in chapter 4:16, 'God is love.' We hear it at weddings; we see it on posters outside churches; it's even thrown at us by sceptics when tragedy strikes: 'I can't believe in a God of love who allows innocent people to die in train crashes and earthquakes.' It seems almost everyone knows it, even those who don't like it: God is love.

But here's the thing for us this evening – the great truth that God is love points us towards the Trinity. For 1 John 4:16 doesn't simply say that God loves, although that is true. And this verse doesn't just say that God is capable of love or that he has the capacity to love, although that is true. And crucially, this verse doesn't say that God became love. No, it says that he *is* love. In his very nature and being, God is love and always has been love. He was love before the creation of the universe. And in order to be love, before anything was created, he must have loved within himself.

In his excellent book, *The Good God*,[4] Mike Reeves introduces us to Richard of St Victor, who lived and died in the twelfth century. Richard understood that for God to be love he must be more than one person. He argued that if God was just one person, he could not be intrinsically loving, since for all eternity (before creation) he would have nobody to love. And then Richard went further. He explained that if there were two persons in the godhead, then God might be loving, but not with a purity of love that exists between three. For in a relationship of two, God's love might be exclusive and ungenerous. So he argued that being perfectly loving, from all eternity, the Father and the Son have delighted to share their love with and through the Holy Spirit.

This great truth we know and cherish that God is love tells us that God is not just one person on his own. And that in turn is very important, because it tells us crucial things about the creation. First, understanding that God is love – in a loving relationship within himself – knocks on the head the idea that God created the universe and created us because he needed someone to love. God – Father, Son and Holy Spirit – existed and lived together in glorious, loving, harmonious unity for eternity, before the universe began. To explain this, C. S. Lewis wrote that 'God is not static, but dynamic; the Trinity pulsates with life in a kind of dance.'[5] I love that thought, because it tells us that, before the creation of the world, before anything else existed, God wasn't just sitting on his throne, static, lonely and wondering what to do. No, Father, Son and Spirit were loving the other, focusing their attention on the other, adoring and serving the other, glorifying the other.

And so, Tim Keller writes,

> Because the Father, Son and Spirit are giving glorifying love to one another, God is infinitely, profoundly happy. Think about this: If you find somebody you adore, someone for whom you would do anything, and you discover that this person feels the same way about you, does that feel good? It's sublime! That's what God has been enjoying for all eternity. The Father, the Son and the Spirit are pouring love and joy and adoration into the other, each one serving the other. They are infinitely seeking one another's glory, and so God is infinitely happy.[6]

God doesn't need us to be happy. And that is very important to know. When God loves us, he doesn't love because he needs someone to love or someone to love him back; his love for us is a pure love.

Also, this truth that God is love and loving within himself tells us that loving relationships are at the heart of the universe. The world that God made reflects the God that he is. We were made in God's image. God is love and so at the heart of the universe is love and loving relationships – that's why loneliness is so devastating and so destructive; that's why we can't live solitary lives that are meaningful and satisfying; that's why we need to love and to be loved. But then we know that deep down. That's what our hearts are longing for, and it all stems from the Trinity.

God the Father

1 John 3:1 speaks of the love of the Father. Now please, when we read in the Bible that God is the Father, we must not think that this is an illustrative description. The declaration, 'God the Father', is *not* a description telling us that God just acts like a Father, as if God thought to himself, 'How can I explain to human beings what I'm like? Oh, I know, every human being has a father. I'll say that I'm like a father.' That's *not* it.

When the Bible refers to God the Father, it is not just telling us that he acts like a Father, but that he *is* the Father. Indeed, rather than God acting like human fathers, it's very important that we see it the other way round. God is the Father, and human fathers are supposed to act like him. That's crucial, because over the years I've met people who have found it extraordinarily difficult to relate to God as their heavenly Father, because they have had terrible human fathers.

Many of us have a picture of our earthly fathers in our minds, and then we magnify that picture a million times to get a picture of God. And so, we see in God all the imperfections in our fathers magnified. Then, God the Father seems to be a horrible thing. What we should do is the reverse. We should know that God is the perfect Father, and we earthly fathers are to follow his example. And the example we should follow is the Father's love for the Son.

Now here again, as with our understanding of the truth that 'God is love', so it is with God the Father – it points us towards the Trinity. The very name 'Father' tells us there must be a Son. Quite simply, if there has not always been the Son, then God has not always been the Father. The point is: God didn't become the Father; he is defined as Father, which is very different from human fathers. God has always been the Father.

And the loving relationship between the Father and the Son tells us more about our giving, generous God. As Father, he is one who loves and who loves to give life and blessing to others.

Children of God

I love that word 'lavish' in 1 John 3:1. The love the Father has and gives is a love that is sumptuously rich, elaborate and extravagant. His love is generous, liberal and bountiful.

He is open-handed, showering his children with good gifts. And the extreme lavishness of God's love is seen in him making us children of God. It's hard to believe sometimes that I am a child of God. I am in the family of God, able to enjoy all the family benefits and sure of the family inheritance. And I am loved unconditionally by this God, whose love is like no other.

Wasn't it fantastic to see William and Kate with new baby George last week? How did they describe the experience of becoming parents? They said it was 'emotional' and 'a very special time'. Little George had done nothing, but he was loved. Christian here tonight, you are a child of the King. Not the king of England, but the King of the universe. And that King is a King who is love. You can know that you are loved and you will always be loved, not because God needs you, not because you've done anything to earn or deserve his love, but because you are his child and he is a fantastically loving God. That is what he is like – God is love.

And what an extraordinary love that is when we know what we're like. I am a rebellious sinner and yet I am loved with the same love that the Father had for the Son before the creation of the world. And we see just how great and generous that love is when we look at the cross, for there we see God adopting us as his children. Look with me at 1 John 4:9–10: 'This is how God showed his love among us: he sent his one and only Son into the world that we might live through him. This is love: not that we loved God, but that he loved us and sent his Son as an atoning sacrifice for our sins.' At the cross we see the extent of God's love. The Father sent his Son as an atoning sacrifice for our sins. And we will be blown away by that sacrificial love when we remember that the Father loved the Son with a perfect love from eternity, for eternity.

Seven years ago my mum was seriously ill and we thought she was about to die. My dad sat at her hospital bed and said to me that he wished he could swap places with her. It was harder for him to see her in pain – the wife he had loved for over fifty years – than for him to go through the pain and die himself. If that is the love between a man and his wife, how much more in the Trinity between the Father and the Son where the Father has loved the Son not for fifty years, but for all eternity past? They have never had a cross word; they have always loved each other perfectly. And yet, the Father gave the Son. It was agony for the Father to see the Son die. But he gave his Son so that you and I could become children of God. And remember, he didn't do it because he needed someone to love or needed us to love him. He did it because he is love, because he is the Father and it is in his very nature to love with a pure love that delights in loving others.

Do you know anyone who loves you so much that they would die for you? Maybe you do. It's a wonderful thing. Now let me ask, do you know anyone who you've ignored all your life who would love you enough to die for you? That's the love of God for you. The Father gave his Son, the Son whom he loves with an extraordinary love. He gave his Son so that we can become children of God. And having been on the receiving end of that love, and having been made children of God, that should transform the way we live.

So, John writes in chapter 3:2 that we are children of God, and when Jesus returns we'll be like him, like the Son. We've been adopted as children. We've enjoyed the lavish love of the Father, and we know the Son will return to make us like him. And that hope should change us in two ways. First, we should want to purify ourselves by not sinning: 'Everyone who sins breaks the law; in fact, sin is lawlessness. But you know that he appeared so that he might take away our sins. And in him is no sin. No one who lives in him keeps on sinning. No one who continues to sin has either seen him or known him' (verses 4–6). As a child of God, I should be like the Son of God. The Son loves the Father – he doesn't want to rebel against his Father, he doesn't want to do anything to hurt his Father; he only wants to love his Father and so should we. Having received the Father's love for us, we shouldn't want to hurt him by sinning against him. We should want to love him. Are you struggling with sin, a besetting sin that you can't get rid of? You've tried techniques to try to stop, but it hasn't worked. Well, try this: think on God's love for you and respond to that love by not wanting to hurt the Father who has loved you so much.

And secondly, being a child of God, we should want to love others: 'For this is the message you heard from the beginning: we should love one another' (verse 11). This is where a big chunk of the letter goes from here. My dad died three years ago, but whenever he used to come and visit us and went to church, people who'd never met him before would say to him, 'You're Paul's dad, aren't you? You're so alike.' The same is said of my son Joshua and me. We look alike. Christian, you have been born of God, you're a child of God, and so you should look like your Father. When people look at you, you should look like his Son – not physically, but in character. And God is love, so you and I should be recognized as God's people by the way we love.

Here's where knowing the Trinity transforms us at the most profound level. Do you remember how C. S. Lewis described the relationship in the Trinity like a dance? Tim Keller expands on Lewis's idea by writing,

> A self-centered life is a stationary life; it's static not dynamic. A self-centered person wants to be the centre around which everything else orbits. Picture five people, ten people, a hundred people on a stage together, and everyone of them wants to be the centre. They all just stand there and say to the others, 'You move around me.' And nobody gets anywhere; the dance becomes hazardous, if not impossible.
>
> The Trinity is utterly different. Instead of self-centeredness, the Father, the Son, and the Spirit are characterized in their very essence by mutually self-giving love. No person in the Trinity insists that the others revolve around him; rather each of them voluntarily circles and orbits around the others. If this is ultimate reality, if this is

> what God who made the universe is like, then this truth bristles and explodes with life-shaping, glorious implications for us. If this world was made by a triune God, relationships of love are what life is really all about.[7]

As I've studied the Trinity in these last months, as I've thought about the love the Father has for the Son, as I have thought about the love that he has lavished upon me, I have wanted to love as he loves. Understanding the Trinity changes the way we live and love. It changed Nicky Cruz, a gang warlord, into a loving servant of Jesus Christ.

When I consider the Father who is this generous, I'll be generous. When I think about the Father who sacrificed his Son, I'll be self-giving. When I reflect on the Father who delights to bring life and blessing to others, I'll want to do the same. When I know and think on the God who is love and who has loved me enough to give his precious Son to die for me, to adopt me into his family and make me a child of God, when I know the God who loves like this, I will want to be loving, cultivating warm and lasting friendships, even with people who have not loved me. Now that is supernatural, transforming trinitarian love.

Notes

1. Nicky Cruz, *Run Baby Run* (Hodder & Stoughton, 2003).
2. Fred Sanders, *Embracing the Trinity* (IVP, 2010), p. 32.
3. Ibid., p. 7.
4. Michael Reeves, *The Good God* (Paternoster, 2012).

5. C. S. Lewis, *Mere Christianity* (William Collins, 2012).
6. Timothy Keller, *King's Cross* (Hodder & Stoughton, 2013), pp. 7–8.
7. Ibid., pp. 8–9.

Following the Son

by Mike Hill

Mike Hill has been the Bishop of Bristol since 2003. He became a Christian at the age of eighteen and, after a short career in the printing industry, was ordained in 1977 and served in parish ministry. As Bishop of Bristol, he has held a number of national responsibilities within the Church of England. He is passionate about Christian leadership and is a sought-after speaker and teacher.

Following the Son: Ephesians 2:1–10

Of all the writings of St Paul, I would probably choose Ephesians 2:1–10 should I want an amazing précis of the gospel. In this passage of Scripture, we see Paul taking up two profound gospel themes. He tackles the hopelessness of biblical anthropology, which is what the Bible teaches about the human condition prior to conversion. Then, in contrast, he speaks of the profound hope we have because of the gospel. These are two key themes for the church today in our rampantly secularizing culture.

Biblical anthropology

I have often thought that one of the things that gets in the way of a person becoming a Christian is pride, one of the so-called seven deadly sins, though in the end of course all sin is deadly. Much has been written about how our culture plays the blame game: it's my environment; it's my parents; it's my school; it's my wife/husband; it's always someone else's responsibility. Even the people of God can become adept at the blame game.

In the book of the prophet Ezekiel, we see the nation of Israel playing the blame game. They were going through a torrid time in exile in Babylonia. The temple in Jerusalem lay in ruins, and the spiritual leaders of Israel were in captivity. To explain their lot, they coined a proverb:

> The parents eat sour grapes,
> and the children's teeth are set on edge.
> (Ezekiel 18:2)

What were they saying? The exile is not our fault. It's our forefathers who put us here; we are merely hapless victims. God's response is blunt and certainly to the point: 'As surely as I live, declares the Sovereign LORD, you will no longer quote this proverb in Israel. For every living soul belongs to me, the father as well as the son – both alike belong to me. The soul who sins is the one who will die.'[1] In other words, God says to his people then and today, *you* have to take responsibility for the sin in your life. Don't blame everyone else. The reason I say this is that, before you can know the riches of a life lived in sweet fellowship with God through faith, you have to admit something. Let's note what Paul says about the unredeemed life:

We were dead (verse 1).
We followed the ways of this world (verse 2).
We gratified the cravings of our sinful nature (verse 3).
We followed its desires and thoughts (verse 3b).

We were dead

Well, obviously, this is not literally true. Paul's readers in their pre-conversion state could be considered dead but, literally speaking, they were alive – otherwise they would have found it hard to read his letter! In the splendour of the garden of Eden, the man and the woman were given the freedom of that remarkable beauty spot. Only one thing was forbidden: 'You must not eat fruit from the tree that is in the middle of the garden, and you must not touch it, or you will die' (Genesis 3:3). The rest, as they say, is history. But behind the history is a mystery. The man and woman didn't die. They lived. So what died in that moment? It wasn't their physical lives. No, their relationship with God died. They became spiritually dead. The rest of Genesis 3 records the punishment handed out by God for this disobedience. An unredeemed life is a spiritually dead life. You can have an interest in spiritual things but be spiritually dead, according to Paul. That's why in verse 5 Paul is very keen to affirm that redemption brings us to life spiritually.

We followed the ways of this world

Estranged from God, they were deceived into thinking that they were free to do whatever they wanted. Since then, human beings have believed that true freedom is attained by casting off the restraint of morality. I was a child of the 1960s. This was the crucible in which was mixed much of what is wrong in our society today. The message of the swinging sixties was: cast off morality – it's bad for you; cast off the idea that sexual behaviour is best saved for marriage; cast off any restriction around experimentation with drugs; cast off talk of responsibilities – we'll fight for our rights now; and even cast off your underwear as a symbol of the new freedom you have found.

We gratified the cravings of our sinful nature

We read in verse 2 of the consequence of this web of lies. We simply live to gratify the cravings of our sinful nature. We begin to live little better than animals. We become carnal, and you don't have to look far into our culture to evidence just that: broken homes, broken lives and broken children.

We followed its desires and its thoughts

Finally, Paul describes us as following the desires and thoughts of our sinful nature (verse 3b). Of course, today our culture is full of distraction. We have never been able to access so much information via the World Wide Web. We, as a culture, have never been so subjected to the mind-changing techniques of sophisticated marketing. We get emails and text messages that many of us seem compelled to answer there and then. This stuff can play with your mind, and what plays with your mind will impact on your behaviour. I imagine that Paul knew very little about neuroscience and behavioural psychology, but he did know that there is a connection between thoughts and behaviours: 'Finally, brothers and sisters, whatever is true, whatever is noble, whatever is right, whatever is pure, whatever is lovely, whatever is admirable – if anything is excellent or praiseworthy – think about such things' (Philippians 4:8). I wish there was more time to talk about this, but let me simply say that I think we are naive about what we put into our minds. We need to be more protecting of ourselves. This is really just being smart about not putting yourself in the way of temptation.

So, to end this section of our passage, we need to deal with a tricky subject for many. 'Like the rest, we were by nature objects of wrath' (verse 3).[2] Debate has raged around this word translated as 'wrath' or 'anger'. Many modern commentators don't like the word at all. This is evidenced by theologians like C. H. Dodd, who could not consider the idea of wrath or anger being ascribed to God. Although we can't jettison the concept – the word occurs eleven times in Paul's letter to the Romans – it is understandable why some are so nervous of speaking about God's wrath.

In part, this is because anger in human beings is somewhat random. Something that doesn't make us mad today may well do tomorrow. Let me say that it is very dicey to interpret a quality we see in ourselves and ascribe our experience of that quality to God. It would not work for qualities such as mercy and grace, and it will not do simply to write off a biblically ascribed quality such as wrath. To put it simply, and I hope not irreverently, God does not have 'bad-hair days'. We do!

John Stott said that we need to be more grateful to God for his wrath, because he always reacts to evil in the same unchanging, predictable, uncompromising way. Without his moral constancy, we'd have no peace. Tom Wright has also made the point that, if God didn't get angry when he saw people being hurt, he couldn't be loving. If God saw us lying, cheating and abusing one another and said, 'Never mind, I love you all anyway', he'd be neither good nor loving.

Another snare that has divided evangelical theologians is the caution around the words 'objects of wrath' or, as it is more frequently translated, 'children of wrath'. As it happens, I think the context here is specific and refers to the pre-Christian status of the believers he is writing to. Of course, debate has formed around whether sweet little babies are under God's wrath from day one. The phrase 'by nature' would suggest something more than a simple propensity to sin. We shall not know this side of heaven quite what Paul meant here, and sadly, I can't go into the very elaborate arguments that history has bequeathed to us. They align around two apparently polar positions:

- We are born with a tendency towards sin; we all therefore do sin and that brings us under the judgment of God.

- We are, from a spiritual point of view, genetically sinners, and our very being as humans from the moment we arrive from the womb is under God's judgment.

Although the Westminster Confession and the Thirty-Nine Articles of Religion of the Church of England, Reformed confessions, strongly teach the latter position, it can be said that most Protestant theologians believe that God's grace and atonement cover the years of childhood until the age of responsibility. And those within the Reformed tradition have relied on the biblical evidence that the children of Christian parents are born within the covenant. What we must repudiate as evangelicals are those who deny the very idea of the wrath of God because it doesn't fit in with their vague ideas about God. God made man in his own image; we must avoid the tendency to remake him in ours!

The optimism of the believer

Well, we've talked about the diagnosis of the unbeliever; we now turn to the cure, wonderfully captured in verses 8 and 9. Before this, however, Paul reminds us of three things: the motive, the message and the method of God's divine plan

The motive of God's divine plan

Verse 4 says, 'Because of his great love for us' – everything God does he does because he loves us. He hates our sin but he still loves us, as Paul says in Romans 5:8: 'While we were still sinners, Christ died for us.' The grace of God means he shows his love to us, even though we don't deserve it. In his Gospel, John tells us, 'God so loved the world that he gave his one and only Son' (John 3:16). Why the incarnation? Because God loves you. Why the cross? Because God loves you. Why the resurrection? Because God loves you. Why will you share his glory? Because God loves you. The whole unfolding message of salvation in the Bible is driven by this God of love, this God of truly amazing grace.

The message of God's divine plan

In verses 5 and 6 there are three verbs to note: God made us alive with him (Jesus), God raised us up with him and God made us sit with him. What is optimistic for the believer about these phrases is that what God did to Jesus in the resurrection, ascension and the session, he does to us. Incidentally, the word 'session' is simply an archaic word for 'sitting', and describes the fact, as is contained in the Apostles' Creed, that after his ascension Jesus was exalted to the right hand of God.

Paul has already told the believers in chapter 1 that God has blessed them in the heavenly realms with every spiritual blessing in Christ. And here Paul spells out what those blessings are: God made us alive with Jesus, God raised us up with Jesus and God made us sit with Jesus.

Some years ago there was a TV programme called the *Beverly Hillbillies*. This was a story about a poverty-stricken farming family from somewhere in the deep south of

North America who discovered oil on their little homestead. Overnight they were fabulously rich. They moved to a mansion in Beverly Hills, hence the title of the programme. The problem is that, if you're not used to wealth and sophistication, much of what you confront is very confusing. For instance, they puzzled while in the billiard room why their dining table had six nets on it! In the end they settled for living in the kitchen. They had a mansion, but they lived in one room. We have been blessed with every spiritual blessing in Christ, but sometimes I think Christians, metaphorically speaking, live in the kitchen. If you're a believer, you are 'in Christ'. We are not just people who worship Jesus or say the Creeds, though we are those people, but what is distinctive is this idea that we are united with him. And God's purpose is that in the coming days we will be shown the incomparable riches of his grace. We think that we have already received the riches of his grace through his life, death and resurrection, but there's more to come.

The method of God's divine plan

So we come to the succinct statement in verses 8 and 9 of how we become Christians. It is by grace – *sola gratia*. Paul, emphasizing the gracious initiative of God, tells us that this is God's gift. What amazes me is how many people sit in churches year after year and apparently don't get the gospel. Of course, this is likely in a church which doesn't proclaim the gospel, but even in some of our evangelical churches there are souls who are still hoping that, by their works, they have done enough to get into heaven. They say, 'I've tried my best . . . I've lived a good life.' But Paul very clearly states here in verse 9, 'not by works, so that no one can boast'. There is nothing you can do to save yourself. That's what we used to call the doctrine of the total depravity of man. It is God who saves by his amazing grace.

If you're trusting in your good works to get you into heaven, you will be a spiritual neurotic. You will never have assurance of salvation, never know if you have done enough good works. Very likely you will be scared of dying, because without assurance you are uncertain what the outcome of your life will be.

Verses 8 and 9 are truly the antidote. If the very notion that you can be confident in your salvation sounds like a terrible arrogance, then you probably don't understand the gospel. If salvation was dependent on my good works, it certainly would be arrogance, but precisely because it's wholly a work of grace, it's nothing to do with what I have done – it's all to do with what God has done for me. On that basis, it's almost arrogance not to have assurance!

But finally, Paul says, 'We are God's workmanship, created in Christ Jesus to do good works, which God prepared in advance for us to do.'[3] This almost seems like a contradiction. Having told us that good works won't get us into heaven, Paul now tells us that we were created for good works. Is this a conflicted statement? Well, of course it isn't. What Paul is doing here is making an important distinction. He is saying that we are not saved by our good works, but we are saved *for* good works. John Stott explained that good works are indispensable to salvation, not as its grounds or means, but as its consequence and evidence.

We are God's workmanship. The word can mean masterpiece or work of art. The God who creates us through the gospel re-creates us, and we are his masterpiece. I think we need to remind ourselves of that truth, not as some flimsy self-esteem exercise, but as a fact. When God looks at you, he sees his work of art. Isn't that amazing?

Obscured by the NIV translation is the fact that at the beginning and end of this passage is a verb. In verse 2, the phrase, the 'transgressions and sins, in which you used to live', can be translated 'the sins in which you once walked'. Similarly, in verse 10 the NIV obscures the verb 'walked', by speaking of the 'good works, which God prepared in advance for us to do'. Again, this can be translated 'good works that we should walk in them'. The same verb, but very different concepts – walking in our sin at the beginning of our passage, and walking out our divine calling in the last verse. One is a bowed, stooped walk with a clumsy gait. The other is a confident stride, with the assurance of sins forgiven and a new life of eternal significance.

My impression is there are people in our churches whose gait is closer to the beginning of the chapter than that described in verse 10. The difference is a basic understanding of the gospel. The operating principle of religion is that if I try a little harder, if I clock in at church occasionally, if I do a bit for charity, God will hand me a gold watch for service. The operating principle of the gospel starts with the recognition that I am a miserable sinner and I cannot save myself. Therefore, I need to come to the God of grace, who put his Son on the cross so my sins may be forgiven and I might be saved from the coming wrath.

> Bearing shame and scoffing rude,
> In my place condemned He stood.
> Sealed my pardon, with His blood,
> Hallelujah! What a Saviour![4]

I started out by telling you that one of the biggest stumbling blocks in a human heart is pride: the pride that refuses to acknowledge my sin; the pride that wants to hide from my fellow human beings and from God; the pride that sits in church for years and has never understood the gospel but doesn't want to admit it. Friend, this world needs that gospel. This world needs a people who will preach it and a people who will live it. This world needs you, the new community of God's believers, to be a gospel people. Who will stand for Jesus and his gospel tonight?

Notes

1. NIV 1984.
2. NIV 1984.
3. NIV 1984.
4. P. P. Bliss, 'Man of Sorrows'.

Walking in the Spirit

by Paul Mallard

Paul Mallard has been engaged in full-time Christian ministry for thirty-one years, serving two churches. He is currently the Director of Training and Development for the Midland's Gospel Partnership. He is married to Edrie, and they have four children and four grandchildren.

Walking in the Spirit: Galatians 5:13–26

If you have a Bible, turn to Galatians 5:13–26. The Holy Spirit is mentioned seven times in this passage, and the climax comes right at the end in verse 25, where Paul says, 'Since we live by the Spirit, let us keep in step with the Spirit.' That's our theme tonight: how do we keep in step with the Spirit, why is it important, what does it look like, what does it mean for our individual lives? So let's turn to the Word of God; let's see what God has to say to us this evening. As we look at verses 13–29, I suggest that it tells us four things: there is a clarification, a command, a contrast and a call.

A clarification

Number one: there is a clarification (verses 13–15). Look at verse 13: 'You, my brothers and sisters, were called to be free.' In the book of Galatians Paul is fighting against legalism. Legalism is the idea that somehow I have to earn God's favour by the things I do, that God's love to me depends upon my performance. The issue then was circumcision. God can't love you unless you are circumcised. And Paul responds with all guns blazing: 'No, the grace of God is such that God loves you because you are in Christ. Don't go back. Don't give up your freedom.' When he comes to chapter 5, Paul is still making that same argument: 'It is for freedom that Christ has set us free. Stand firm, then, and do not let yourselves be burdened again by a yoke of slavery' (Galatians 5:1). Don't go back; you are free in Christ. Don't go back to the spirit of slavery.

Legalism is always trying to impose itself upon us, me included. We want to earn some merit, some favour with God, and we are always lapsing into legalism. One of my heroes was the great Baptist preacher, Charles Haddon Spurgeon. I read somewhere that Spurgeon prayed in the morning for twenty minutes. So, I thought, 'If Spurgeon prayed for twenty minutes, I'll pray for twenty minutes.' One morning I was praying and I looked at my clock and I'd been praying for twenty-two minutes, and I thought, 'Boy, I've got to be really spiritual, praying more than Spurgeon.' The problem was the next morning if I only made eighteen minutes, then God couldn't possibly love me and bless me as much as he had the previous day. That's the way we work, isn't it? Paul says, 'No, don't go back to that. God has set you free from legalism – you are free.'

Paul says, 'Do not use your freedom to indulge the sinful nature; rather, serve one another humbly in love.' Can you see what he is saying? 'Don't lose your freedom, but don't abuse your freedom.' Here's the danger: if God has made me free and his love doesn't depend upon my performance, does that mean I can do anything? Paul says, 'No, don't use it as an excuse to gratify the desires of the sinful nature.' In some of your versions, verse 13 will say 'desires of the flesh'. The flesh is the old sinful nature that we were born with; it's what we were before we came to know Christ. We were all originally born in the flesh; it's our fallen, corrupt, sinful nature – the old nature without Christ. Paul says, don't give in to that; instead, serve one another in love. The word 'serve' in Greek is derived from the same word as *doulos*. *Doulos* means 'being a slave'. Be a slave to one another. God set you free from the slavery of the law. Why? So that you may enter into the slavery of love.

I remember a distinct moment when I lost my freedom. At 11.30 on the 8 August 1979, I was a free man, absolutely free as a bird. I went to a church – I'd put on a suit which was very rare for me – I saw an angel moving down the aisle, I said, 'I do'. I went into the back, I signed in blood and I lost my freedom. I became a slave, a slave of love. In a few days' time it will be the thirty-fourth year of my slavery. I tell you, I am the happiest slave who has ever walked the face of the earth. Many years earlier, I became a slave of Jesus Christ. And now I want to please him, not to earn his favour, but because I love him. The Spirit moves within my heart; he shows me Jesus and he ignites my heart with love for Jesus. But that's the easy bit.

The next bit is the difficult bit. Look at the next verse: 'The entire law is fulfilled in keeping this one command: "Love your neighbour as yourself"' (verse 14). You see, loving Jesus is easy because he is lovable. Loving the people of Jesus is a bit more difficult, isn't it? Look what was happening with the Galatians: 'If you keep on biting and devouring each other, watch out or you will be destroyed by each other.' Paul was saying, 'You may have wonderful theological ideas, but you are at one another's throats, you're biting like animals, you're destroying one another.' A mark of the work of the Spirit within us is a love for Christ, but you cannot love Christ without loving his people. This passage is about holiness, and personal holiness is *always* within the context of loving the people of God.

Turn to Ephesians 4:29–31:

> Do not let any unwholesome talk come out of your mouths, but only what is helpful for building others up according to their needs, that it may benefit those who listen. And do not grieve the Holy Spirit of God, with whom you were sealed for the day of redemption. Get rid of all bitterness, rage and anger, brawling and slander, along with every form of malice.

The single most important thing I can say to you about the Holy Spirit is this: the Holy Spirit is not a force, not an *it*, not a thing, not a power, not a commodity. The Holy Spirit is a person, a divine person, a holy person, a gracious person and a gentle person. Maybe you don't think of him like that, but you need to start. You need to think of the fact that the Spirit can be grieved. Grieving is a love word – you realize that, don't you? Don't say that the Spirit will be angry; rather, the Spirit will be grieved by your sin. Galatians talks about what grieves the Holy Spirit: bitterness, anger, rage, slander. Think about your relationship with people in your church; think what that relationship is like and how it affects your relationship with the Holy Spirit.

A command

Number two: there is a command: 'So I say, live by the Spirit, and you will not gratify the desires of the sinful nature' (Galatians 5:16). Paul is now going to talk about the power of the work of the Spirit within our lives. He is going to mention the Spirit seven times in ten verses: live by the Spirit; be led by the Spirit; the Spirit yearns within us; the Spirit produces fruit in us; the Spirit keeps us in step and we have to keep in step with him; live by the Spirit and you will not gratify the desires of the sinful nature.

But Paul is being incredibly realistic about the Christian life. He is describing your life and my life this evening. 'For the sinful nature, the flesh, the self-centred nature, desires what is contrary to the Spirit' (verse 17). The word 'desire' literally means 'yearn with a passion'. That old nature is still within us, yearning with a passion, and you know what it's yearning for? Everything that is against the Spirit, and the Spirit is yearning with a passion for everything that is against the sinful nature. Tonight, my friend, you are a walking civil war if you are a Christian. You know within your hearts that there is a battle raging, a battle between two forces yearning for very opposite things: your old nature and the living Spirit of God with whom you were sealed against the day of redemption.

Let me tell you about Dave. Dave was one of the very first converts in my first church. He was a rough bloke: he worked in a factory, he got into fights on a Saturday night and he walked past our church to buy a *News of the World* every Sunday. And then one day he came in. Dave's language was ripe, but he came under conviction of sin and wanted to be saved. He said, 'Pastor, I don't know what to do. I can't stop swearing. I've decided I'm going to wait until I stop swearing, then I'm going to become a Christian.' I said, 'Dave, you can't wait until you stop swearing, or you will never come. Come to Jesus as you are, and I promise you he will clean up your mouth.' And he was saved, wonderfully saved. Six months after his conversion, he came to me in tears: 'Pastor, I've blown it.' He was working in a factory on nights and somebody said something about Jesus, and he gave him a mouthful. He said, 'I just want to follow Jesus. I love Jesus, but there is something inside me that is always taking me in the opposite direction. I don't know what it is, but I can't possibly be a Christian, because there are two things fighting away.' And I said, 'Dave, welcome to the club, mate, because that is what it is to be a Christian.'

You know that, don't you? The old nature yearns, the Spirit yearns, and they go at it hammer and tongs, and sometimes you give in to the old nature, and even tonight you've given in to the old nature and you feel wretched. There is a battle going on, but God doesn't leave us high and dry. Look at what Paul says in verse 18: 'But if you are led by the Spirit, you are not under the law.' You are not under the old law dragging you down; you have a new power within you, the active living personal power of God. What does it mean to be led? It means someone is standing beside you and taking you along the way. Who is that person? He is the *ruach*, the *pneuma*, the life of God, the wind of God, the breath of God, the visible, dynamic, life-giving power of God, and ultimately he will always beat the flesh. That's good news, isn't it?

A contrast

Number three: in verses 19–23 there is a contrast. Paul describes what the flesh yearns for and what the Spirit yearns for. We've got these two powers at work within us. Look at verses 19–21: the flesh yearns for this ugly catalogue of fifteen despicable sins. We can divide them into four groups: sins of sexuality, sins of spirituality, social sins, and the two right at the end are sins of substance abuse. Let's just work through them briefly. The first three in verse 19 are sins of sexuality. Sexual immorality literally means unlawful sex, sex outside the covenant of marriage. Sex was designed by God to be experienced between one man and one woman in a covenant for life, and any sex outside of that is unlawful sex.

The second word is impurity or uncleanness: it actually means unnatural sex. In Greek it's a word that has its origins in the medical profession, used to describe the puss that comes out of a putrefying wound – it's vile and horrible. Paul didn't know about the pornography which is flooding our nation, but that's what he is talking about. The third sin is debauchery, which actually means reckless sex that is unlawful, unnatural and uncontrollable. Sex is a gift of God within marriage and it is a good gift. God invented it. So we are not saying that sex inside marriage is wrong – just the opposite. It's the flesh taking it and misusing it that is wrong.

Look at the next two sins. These are sins of spiritual idolatry and witchcraft, both of which are attempts to control God. Next are social sins in verses 20–22, and here is where the rubber hits the road. We'd be a little bit shocked if the first five sins occurred in our church. But hatred, discord, jealousy, fits of rage and selfish ambition and dissensions, factions and envy – Paul, have you been to our church business meeting? Have you seen those things? Those are what someone has described as the 'respectable sins'. Remember, Ephesians, these are the sins that grieve the Holy Spirit. Lastly, substance abuse, drunkenness and orgies: anyone who continues in those sins without being horrified and wanting to turn from them will not enter the kingdom of God (verse 21).

What about the fruit of the Spirit? The first three are to do with our relationship with God: love, joy and peace. The next three are to do with people: patience, kindness and goodness. The last three are inner virtues: faithfulness, gentleness and self-control.

What I want you to notice is that one list is the *works* of the flesh; the other list is the *fruit* of the Spirit. Although you've got an old nature, maybe you do bad things; the old nature is doing works, but that is not you – you are a new creation in Christ. What defines you is your new nature and the power and the presence of the Holy Spirit. What defines you is the fruit of the new nature coming out. And here's the great truth – in the end, by the power of God, that sinful nature will be destroyed, but not in this life; there's no such thing as sinless perfection. So that's the contrast.

A call

We've come to the last section (verses 24–26). Here is a call to do something, and it's a negative and a positive. The first call is negative: 'Those who belong to Christ Jesus have crucified the sinful nature with its passions and desires' (verse 24). If we are Christians, we have a call to put to death that sinful nature. We do it in the power of the Spirit (Romans 8), but the ball is in our court – we have to do something about it.

Last year I was preaching in Buckie in the North of Scotland, and one afternoon a guy took me out on a boat. He'd been a crab fisherman all his life. He was pulling up crabs. The little crabs he threw back into the sea, but occasionally these great big monsters came out. They were twice the size of my fist, with these great snappers. I noticed how gingerly he was handling them and I said, 'You are being very careful!' 'Oh,' he said, 'I've seen men caught by a crab in its clutches. It gets you between its pincers, and if it's got your finger it will not let you go. I've seen a man have his finger broken by a crab.' I asked him, 'What do you do if you've got a crab on your finger?' He said, 'You walk to the side of the boat and you smash it. The crab won't let go of you until you've destroyed it. If you don't destroy it, it will break your finger.' If you don't deal seriously with sin, sin will deal seriously with you. That's what the old Puritans meant when they spoke about mortification: you put sin to death, kill it. There are people sitting in this tent tonight who are giving in to that sinful nature, and tonight you need to make a decision before God to break that sin and to deal with it once and for all, to smash it, put it to death, crucify it.

That's the negative. Now look at the positive in verse 25. We are not supposed to deal with sin just in our own strength. 'Since we live by the Spirit, let us keep in step with the Spirit.' What does it mean to 'keep in step with the Spirit'? In means two things: to follow his directions and depend upon his help. Follow his directions in the Word. If we want to be led by the Spirit, we have to be in the

Word. He'll hide the Word in your heart, he'll bring the Word to your attention, he'll remind you in your conscience and he will use the Word to transform you. Being led by the Spirit comes through immersing ourselves in the living Word of God. To be led by the Spirit is to be controlled by the Word of God, to be filled with Scripture.

The second thing it means is to depend by faith on his strength. God is living in us, and that power of God is a life-transforming power. This person has come into your life with an agenda, and it's an agenda for change. He's powerful, he's wonderful, he created the world, he turned chaos to cosmos and he can turn the chaos of your life into cosmos. And so, Paul says, 'Live in the light of that.' Look at the last verse (26): 'Let us not become conceited, provoking and envying each other.' In other words, live in the power of the Spirit.

As we finish, let me make three brief applications. Number one: are you a Christian? Is there something strange within your heart that is beginning to drive you to things you've never seen before, something that is making Jesus attractive? That is the work of the Holy Spirit. Is the Spirit at work within you tonight? Respond to that; talk and pray with someone. Tonight would be a wonderful night to come to God and to receive forgiveness and the gift of the Spirit. Number two: if you are a Christian and you are struggling with sin, is tonight the night where you draw a line through it? If the Holy Spirit has spoken to you about pornography, bitterness of heart, unkindness or forgiveness, deal with it tonight, go and pray with someone.

Number three: if you are a Christian, you may say, 'I just want God to fill me afresh with his Spirit, I want to love Jesus more by the power of his Spirit, I want to follow Jesus, I want the Spirit to make Jesus more beautiful and I want my life to be more holy, more pure.' Here we are in the middle of the week. Tonight may well be the night you need to deal with something significant and important in your life. Respond to the work of the Holy Spirit – adorable, wonderful, beautiful and glorious – the Spirit of the living God.

People of the Trinity – Unity in Diversity

by Richard Condie

Richard Condie has been Vicar of St Jude's Anglican Church, Carlton, in Melbourne, Australia for the past eleven years. St Jude's is a church of 600 meeting in seven different congregations, working to reach tertiary students, young workers, families, migrants and refugees with the gospel of Christ. Prior to St Jude's, Richard taught New Testament at Ridley, Melbourne. He is married to Helen and they have two teenage children. He also serves as Archdeacon of Melbourne.

People of the Trinity – Unity in Diversity: Ephesians 4:1–16

Samuel Stone knew his Bible well when he wrote the magnificent hymn, 'The Church's One Foundation':

> The Church's one foundation
> Is Jesus Christ her Lord;
> She is His new creation
> By water and the Word.
> From heaven He came and sought her
> To be His holy bride;
> With His own blood He bought her,
> And for her life He died.

The verse is riddled with biblical imagery and allusions; it's wonderful theology in song. In fact, this is one of twelve hymns Samuel Stone wrote to instruct his congregation in the tenets of the Apostles' Creed. One English archbishop is quoted as saying that, whenever he was called upon to open or dedicate a church, he could always count on two things: cold chicken and 'The Church's One Foundation'.

But Samuel Stone also knew the church well: her life and witness, warts and all. Listen to the first lines of verse three:

> Though with a scornful wonder
> Men see her sore oppressed,
> By schisms rent asunder,
> By heresies distressed.

We wonder at the glory of the church, but despair when we see the divisions, the breakdown of relationships and the pain of disunity. Spats between different factions and within denominations are common. And at a personal level, if you have been a Christian a little while, then you almost certainly will know what I mean. Barely is there a church without a story of broken relationships, major conflict, diverse and divergent directions. So, who am I tonight to be speaking about unity? Is it just pie in the sky, a lovely notion but largely unachievable? Or is it something else altogether?

My talk tonight is in four major sections. First, let's look at:

Our unity (verses 1–6)

This is the section of Paul's letter where he begins to apply all that he has said in chapters 1 – 3 about the glory of the gospel to the lives of those in the Ephesian church. Verse 1 says, 'As a prisoner for the Lord, then, I urge you to live a life worthy of the calling you have received.' This is a topic sentence for all that flows in the next three chapters. And so, what we have here builds on the theological presentation of chapters 1 – 3, and there are some wonderful things to learn there about our trinitarian life. Fortunately, Peter Baker spoke from Ephesians 2, and we'll finish our evening series in two nights' time by looking at Ephesians 3. So tonight we can concentrate on this theme of unity.

Paul wants the Ephesians to know and to live out the foundations of their unity in God who is Father, Son and Spirit. As he does this, he begins with four graces that he expects to see as a result of how Christ has treated them with his grace, mercy and love that broke down the walls of division in the early church. Look with me at verse 2: 'Be completely humble and gentle; be patient, bearing with one another in love.' The Father's love for the Son in 1:6 and the Father's love for us in 1:4; 2:4; and 3:17 now becomes the model for Christian living. His love replaces our base motives with humility, gentleness, patience and love, and they set the scene for a wonderful treatment of unity.

Let's read on: 'Make every effort to keep the unity of the Spirit through the bond of peace. There is one body and one Spirit, just as you were called to one hope when you were called; one Lord, one faith, one baptism; one God and Father of all, who is over all and through all and in all' (verses 3–6). Now I hope when you heard the seven 'ones', you heard very clearly the three persons of the one essence of God: one Spirit, one Lord, one Father, and then four spheres of his work associated with each person of the Trinity. One body and one hope associated with the Spirit, one faith and one baptism associated with the Lord, and the reign of God the Father over all. It is a very striking and powerful list showing the unity of the Spirit that we have.

One Spirit: the Holy Spirit who beckons each of us into the life of the body, who creates and binds us together. One body: one universal, catholic church – that is the invisible church of God to which we all belong as followers of Christ – and in the Ephesian context, especially the church that brings Jew and Gentile together. One hope: the sure goal of our faith, the resurrection from the dead that is the universal promise to all God's children. One Lord: the Lord Jesus Christ's death paves the way for every Christian believer; he is the one way to the Father. And his work is illustrated by one faith, here probably meaning the body of belief, the substance of what is believed about Jesus, the faith handed down to us. And one baptism: here a reference to the same sacrament by which every believer has his or her entry into the family signified. And the one God and Father of us all: God the Father, who is supreme and transcendent, over all, pervasive and immanent, through all and in all. It's quite a statement, isn't it? These things are true of every believer.

At St Jude's we are blessed with a great diversity of people. Our main church building sits a block from Melbourne University, a block from a retail and Italian dining precinct, and across the road from a large public housing estate with 6,000 residents, many refugees and people with mental illness.

Doris is a member of our church. She is old, disabled and lives off a pension. She has suffered much of her life, had very low education and has very little money, but she is a regular at worship and Bible study each week. Tim could not be more different. He is a professor of international law at Melbourne University and a special advisor to the International Court in The Hague. He is an educated, articulate citizen of the world. Amir[1] is a recently arrived refugee from Iran. He speaks very little English, came on a leaky boat from Indonesia and was held in immigration detention on Christmas Island where he heard the gospel for the first time. Through lots of translation and Bible study in Farsi, he became a believer and was recently baptized. Zichao is a smart young Chinese Singaporean student who gave his life to Christ at St Jude's. He was baptized and now serves in a church on the other side of the city.

The miracle is that Doris, Tim, Amir and Zichao are brothers and sister in Christ, held together in an unshakable and indissoluble unity of one body, one Spirit, one hope, one Lord, one faith, one baptism and one God and Father of them all. And that's what binds you and me together too! Even though we have never met, we are brothers and sisters in Christ, united to one another.

But what of the third verse of Samuel Stone's hymn? Is this just a glorious fiction of the apostle Paul, a figment of his imagination to speak of unity in such glowing terms when our experience of the church is 'by schisms rent asunder, by heresies distressed'? Well, I jumped over a verse, didn't I? Verse 3 says, 'Make every effort to keep the unity of the Spirit through the bond of peace.' You see, there is an objective reality to our unity: the seven 'ones' in the invisible, eternal church, seen by God in the heavens, unified by one Spirit, body, hope, Lord, faith, baptism, God and Father of us all. But we must *make every effort* to keep that unity. The words have an urgency to them in the original Greek, the air of an impending crisis. We are charged to make every effort to keep the unity of the Spirit evident, transparent and real in our relationships.

You can't hear these words and not care about the schisms in your denomination, the quarrels in your local congregation or the falling out between the saints in your neighbourhood. We *have* a great unity by virtue of the trinitarian God, but we are to work at exposing it and living it.

A great threat to unity is brewing and in some ways boiling over in my denomination, and perhaps in yours as well, over human sexuality. I think the heart of the problem, and why it is so damaging, is that it stems from fundamental differences about authority, about the place of the Word of God, disagreement about the one faith and what the one Lord wants for us.

And so, unity is worth fighting for! It's worth making every effort to defend. Those broken relationships in your own church community are worth working at to restore, so that the glorious unity we have in Christ might be shown to the world.

But my second point is:

Our diversity (verses 7–12)

The wonder of this unity is not its uniformity, bland sameness or conformity, but its diversity. Verses 7–12 make this clear. Look at verse 7: 'But to each one of us grace has been given as Christ apportioned it.' We've just had *one, one, one, one, one*; now we have 'to each one'. To each individual that makes up the unity something has been given: a grace, a free underserved gift, so that each might play a part in the unity. There are a number of lists of spiritual gifts in the New Testament – none are the same: some have more gifts, others have less (see 1 Corinthians 12; Romans 12; 1 Peter 4). And this suggests that what we read in Ephesians is not exhaustive.

What each gift actually means is not our primary concern tonight, except to note that each gift listed here is a speaking office, and collectively they have one purpose. The gift of apostles and prophets seems to apply to the foundation period of the church, although some argue that today certain ministries are apostolic and prophetic in nature, even if that is not strictly what is intended here. But the point is that these, with the gifts of evangelist and pastor teacher, are the leadership/word gifts within the body for a particular function.

Please look carefully with me at verse 12. The reigning, ascended Lord Jesus Christ, through his Spirit descending, gave these speaking offices 'to equip his people for works of service, so that the body of Christ may be built up'. Please notice that it does not say, 'to equip his people [comma] for works of service [comma] so that the body of Christ may be built up'. For if it said that, Paul would be teaching a kind clericalism where the teaching ministries equipped and served the people so that the body was built up.

But it actually says, 'to equip his people for works of service [comma] so that the body may be built up'. You see, in some churches there is an expectation that the pastor teacher will do *all* the work of ministry for building up the body of Christ, that they have a job to do and it is to provide a service to the rest of us. But Paul's vision is much more diverse than that. He wants those leadership gifts used to equip *all* of us for works of service, presumably to use the other gifts given to his people, like leadership, administration, service, discernment, giving, faith and so on, so that together we might build up the body of Christ.

At St Jude's we are fortunate to have a large staff team. There are thirteen of us and a number of interns and trainees. And it would be easy to think that these thirteen people did the ministry in our church and that the ministry was done to the people. But at the back of our church we have a photo board of our staff, a picture of each one with their name and role. And across the top it says, 'St Jude's staff – equipping members for ministry'. We know that our job is to release the ministry of the saints. And the ministry of each one is as important for the building of the body as the ministry of the vicar, the other preachers and pastoral workers. As one writer put it, 'The ministry of the officials does not find its fulfilment in their own existence, but only in the activity of preparing others for ministry.'[2]

Paul's vision for the unity of the church is diversity in action. So that Doris, Tim, Amir and Zichao will each take their place, contributing to the health and building up of the whole. Look at the person next to you. He or she has received a gift of grace from the risen Jesus to perform a work of service for the building up of the body of Christ. Wonderful, isn't it? Lean forward and look at the person next to them. They've got one too! Each one playing their vital part in building and growing the wonderful body that is God's church. Now that is pretty diverse, isn't it? Why would God create unity as diverse as this? Surely it would have been easier for our unity if we had simply been just the same as each other. After all, if everyone were the same, surely our unity would be stronger? Well, this takes me to my third point tonight. We are:

A trinitarian people

It is not an accident that God made us this way, because it reflects his own nature. The seven *ones* from verses 4–6 express the unity of the one God. But in those seven *ones* are the three *persons*. We worship God, who is Father, Son and Holy Spirit: one God a unity, three persons a diversity. Each person in the Trinity is distinct from the other, yet of the same essence. He is a God who understands community, because that is who he is, in his essence.

It is little wonder then that we who are his reflect this unity and diversity, because we are a trinitarian people. Without unity we would end up in fragmentation, contradiction and disintegration. Without diversity we would end up in uniformity, lacking in creativity, with no real community at all. So there is a profoundly trinitarian shape to who we are as God's people, reflecting his very nature.

So we come to the final part of our text:

Maturity in unity (**verses 13–16**)

See how the purpose of our diverse gifting comes full circle: 'until we all reach unity in the faith and in the knowledge of the Son of God and become mature, attaining to the whole measure of the fullness of Christ' (verse 13). The gifts of Christ are given to equip the saints for works of service, for the building up of the body *until* this maturity is attained. Collectively, we are en route to this destination. Please notice that the maturity is expressed as 'unity in the faith' and 'unity in the knowledge of Jesus Christ'.

As is so often in the Scriptures, we have an incidence here of the *now* and the *not yet*. We *have* the unity of the Spirit in essence: that is a given because of the one God who gives it. But we are to exercise our diverse gifts until we *attain* that unity in practice. My denomination, and perhaps yours as well, needs to think about this distinction. We play what I like to call 'happy families'. Our bishops speak of unity, and we pretend when we come together that we are on about the same thing. But scratch the surface, and we find deep rifts over fundamental things like the doctrine of Christ's divinity, the reality of the resurrection or the ethical imperatives of the Scriptures for our life and practice.

One leader in the Anglican Church has said we should keep our unity 'by keeping within sight and sound of each other', by which I think he means that we should listen and respect each other's divergent points of view. But I hope you can see that that kind of pretend unity, pretending we are a 'happy family', will never do if we take verse 13 seriously, because the real basis of demonstrated unity is to do with the knowledge of God and the measure of the fullness of Christ.

Look at how the maturity is played out in verses 14–15. Mature unity is doctrinally sound, stable, like solid ground, not like the bucking and rolling of a ship's deck in the storm. That is the foundation. When we consider God's church and 'we see her sore oppressed, by schisms rent asunder, by heresies distressed', as the Samuel Stone hymn so eloquently puts it, we know we need truth with love.

When you meet troubles in your own fellowship, you need truth with love. When we are fighting for the heart and soul of our denominations, we need truth with love. When we are dealing with personal division, we need truth with love. That is the way we will be held together as the body of Christ: 'From him [that is Christ] the whole body, joined and held together by every supporting ligament, grows and builds itself up in love, as each part does its work' (verse 16).

It's a great vision, brothers and sisters. Let us do everything we can to build the unity of God's church with truth and love.

Listen to how Samuel Stone finishes his hymn:

Yet she on earth hath union
With God the Three in One,
And mystic sweet communion
With those whose rest is won,
With all her sons and daughters
Who, by the Master's hand
Led through the deathly waters,
Repose in Eden land.

O happy ones and holy!
Lord, give us grace that we,
Like them, the meek and lowly,
On high may dwell with Thee:
There, past the border mountains,
Where in sweet vales the Bride
With Thee by living fountains
Forever shall abide!

Let's pray that reality for our church.

Notes

1. Name changed to protect security.
2. E. Best, 'Ministry in Ephesians' in *Essays on Ephesians* (T. & T. Clark, 1977), quoted in P. T. O'Brien, *The Letter to the Ephesians* (Eerdmans, 1999), p. 304.

Participating in the Mission of the Trinity

by Rico Tice

Rico Tice was born in Chile in 1966, and grew up in Uganda and Zaire. He was educated in Dorset and spent a gap year as a youth worker in inner-city Liverpool. He then studied history at Bristol University, where he captained the rugby side. Rico was ordained in 1994 and soon after was appointed to the staff team at All Souls as Associate Minister (Evangelism). Rico is National Director of Christians in Sport.

Participating in the Mission of the Trinity: Matthew 28:16–20

Matthew's particular interest is to present the Messiah to the Jewish people. He says, 'This is your King, your Saviour. Here is the one who fulfils all the Old Testament prophecy.' In chapter 1 we have the genealogy reaching right back. In chapter 2 Jesus was born in Bethlehem, as Micah predicted. In chapter 3 John comes as Isaiah predicts: 'A voice of one calling in the wilderness, "Prepare the way for the Lord"' (verse 3). In chapter 4 the words of Isaiah are fulfilled: 'The people living in darkness have seen a great light' (verse 16). Christ is the promised King, and of course King Herod is desperately threatened by this, so in Matthew 2:16 he gives orders to kill all the baby boys in Bethlehem, as Jeremiah had predicted.

So Matthew presents Jesus Christ to the Jewish people as the real King in whom the kingdom of God has come.

And please see what word defines the rule of this King as he commissions his disciples at the end of Matthew's Gospel in 28:18: 'Then Jesus came to them and said, "All authority in heaven and on earth has been given to me."' Matthew is speaking of Christ the King, and the great thing about a true king is that he has authority. And on this mission night, there are five headings that speak of Christ the King's authority.

The King's victory

The first heading is 'The King's victory' (verses 2 and 6). You can't have authority in human affairs without having won for yourself a power base. Napoleon could not declare himself emperor until he had dealt with Wellington at Waterloo. He failed to deal with Wellington, and so he lost his power base and no longer had the authority to be emperor. So what is Jesus' power base? From where does his authority spring? Have a look at Matthew 28:2: 'There was a violent earthquake, for an angel of the Lord came down from heaven and, going to the tomb, rolled back the stone and sat on it.' So, you put Jesus in the grave, but no power can seal it. Verse 6 says, 'He is not here; he has risen, just as he said. Come and see the place where he lay.' So Jesus' enemies did the very worst they could do, which was to kill him and put him in the grave. That's what you do with your enemy if you want to deal with him; you can't do any worse. But it was not sufficient, because Jesus rose from the dead. He conquered the last great enemy, death. He has sprung from the grave and, as a result, has a remarkable power base which is unique in the universe. Furthermore, he can never die again; his authority can never be taken from him: he really is the victorious King.

Robert Mugabe has a power base, but it will disappear when he dies. Vladimir Putin has a power base, but it will disappear when he dies. But Matthew 28:6 says, 'He has risen', and because of that there is victory. Hebrews 2:14–15 says, 'Since the children have flesh and blood, he too shared in their humanity so that by his death he might break the power of him who holds the power of death – that is, the devil – and free those who all their lives were held in slavery by their fear of death.' Brother and sister, I am sure you do fear the process of dying, but Jesus says, 'I will come to you if you are mine and I will escort you and take you to be with me.' What Christ was doing by his death and resurrection was meeting the challenge of his enemy the devil, and robbing him of human beings who are enslaved to death. Now this last enemy of man is dead, and the devil no longer has the last word. This is the King's victory – he has risen and has an eternal power base.

The King's authority

Secondly, we come to the King's authority. Verse 18 says, 'All authority in heaven and on earth has been given to me.' Who has given him this authority? Only the Father could do such a thing. The Father has put Jesus on the throne of the universe, and by his resurrection he is enthroned over all. There is no higher authority than Jesus, and this could not be a greater claim. 'All authority on earth' means that Jesus has the last word in everything you do and say on earth, not just on Sunday morning. He is the supreme authority, even above the authorities which exist naturally in life: the authorities in your job, in the country, in the church, or whatever it may be. All these have their proper place, but he has supreme authority. So, in all you face, you must remember there is no higher authority than Jesus. He is enthroned over all and he says, 'Take heart, I have overcome the world.' His Word has over-arching authority; he has the authority over and above everybody else in your life to send you exactly where he wants. And the proper response to Jesus Christ is: 'I'll go where you want me to go, I'll be what you want me to be and I'll do what you want me to do.' We have no option, and if you don't say those words in your heart, then you are not, in the New Testament sense, a Christian.

Secondly, please note that he has all authority on earth over the nations, which is why he says, 'Go and make disciples of all nations' (verse 19). Modern culture says we must allow people to live under their religions or gods, but Jesus will have none of it. He is Lord and King, and he said all authority is given to him over all the world, and therefore his disciples must go to all nations. So, here is Jesus presenting himself not as head of the Jewish religion, a Western religion or an Eastern religion. No, the religion of Jesus does not come from East or West; it comes from God. 'All authority in heaven and earth has been given to me' (verse 18) – so Jesus claims authority over all the areas of the earth and over all the religions of men.

Now I don't need to tell you how appalling this sounds to the modern mind. But there is no mistaking it: Jesus has authority over you, he has authority over all nations and he therefore has the right to claim them for himself, and he will not allow them to offer their worship to anyone else. So when the sociologists cry out, 'Why should you wretched Christians go into other parts of the world and disturb societies and people? What an extraordinary arrogance it is for you to do that!' Our answer is: 'Well, it would be if verses 18 and 19 were not written in the New Testament: "All authority in heaven and on earth has been given to me. Therefore go and make disciples of all nations."'

So the King's victory over death leads to the King's authority. And now Jesus stands with a few disciples on this mountain top, and he looks over all the nations of the world and he says, 'They belong to me. Go and take them for me.' Of course, as we think of verse 18, we have to repent of our picture of Jesus, for it is far too small and far too culturally domesticated.

The King's seal

The third point is that the King has a seal. Most kings put a seal onto things that belong to them. Here is the seal: 'baptising them in the name of the Father and of the Son and of the Holy Spirit' (verse 19). So what is baptism? Well, it's the gracious gift of the Father through which believers are incorporated by faith into the life, death and resurrection of Jesus, and become part of the forgiven, gifted and sanctified community of the Holy Spirit. And it's very often when this seal is put on that all hell is let loose in non-Christian cultures. Michael came from a strong Muslim Pakistani family, and he was sent to a mission school to get a good education, but not to listen to Bible classes. His family had great authority, but Christ had a greater authority. One night he went to bed with a verse from Scripture in his mind, and without anything really conscious happening he woke up the next morning and realized that he was a Christian. The Lord had done it; the whole world seemed different. His parents could just about manage this news until he came to this country for further education and he got baptized. Then they cut him off completely and they held his funeral.

You see, baptism is the seal or sign that marks a man or a woman off, and it speaks of being incorporated into the worldwide community that owns the name of the Trinity. So, what does that mean for Michael? What comfort is it for him? Well, it's overwhelming. It means the Father, Son and Spirit have each been centring on the other, giving glorifying love to one another since before the beginning of time. Victor Hugo said that life's greatest happiness is to be convinced that you are loved. Well, that is what God has been enjoying for all eternity: the Father, Son and Spirit are pouring love, joy and adoration into the other, each one serving the other. They are infinitely seeking one another's glory, and so God is infinitely happy. It's what C. S. Lewis once called 'a dance',[1] and by grace we are invited into, baptized into, that community of self-giving love, into that dance. Come and live, come and dance!

A disciple is a learner, a person with 'L-plates'. Who is he learning from? Who is his teacher? Well, the answer is, the triune God is your teacher. We are baptized into the name of the Trinity, so everyone's chief allegiance is to God. When you are baptized into the Trinity, you profess that you are a Christian. That's what we are, and it has reference to the universal church of Christ, but baptism also means joining a local church. You see, you can't be baptized into the air or in theory or by reading a theological textbook. No, somebody has got to take water and apply it to you, and therefore it's done in the local Christian community. I can't own the universal church but not the local church. In the standing orders of Matthew 28, if you don't belong to a local church, it's time you did. If you are a Christian, your loyalty is to the universal church and to the local church. We are to love the local church.

The King's commission and his commandments

It leads fourthly to the King's commission and his commandments. The King's commandments to his local and universal church are very striking. Look down to verse 20: 'teaching them to obey everything I have commanded you'. Now, it's significant that the ministry of these eleven disciples is to be a teaching ministry. It's not a priestly ministry; it's not a sacramental ministry, although they do baptize. It is primarily a matter of preaching and teaching, because the title of Christian is that of disciple, and we are not to teach people theoretically, but so that they actually obey what Christ has commanded.

The church is given the whole Bible and told to go to the whole world. Evangelism according to our Lord Jesus means making disciples so they give their allegiance to him. Secondly, here it is baptism into the Christian church, so they have a local church. And thirdly, it's 'teaching them to obey everything I have commanded you' (verse 20). You know, brothers and sisters, I am so glad these are orders, because so often I don't feel like going. If I listened to my feelings, I would always be waiting to love people more, waiting to feel better equipped or more confident. But here the Lord has commanded us to go and do certain things, and therefore the only issue is: 'Am I willing to do it?'

Brothers and sisters, I am so grateful to the nineteen-year-old who opened the Bible with me for the first time. He was the son of my godfather, who had been killed in a cliff fall. I was nowhere spiritually, and between sets of tennis this nineteen-year-old said to me, 'Would you like to look at the Bible with me?' I said, 'OK'. He opened up the Bible to a text I'll never forget: Psalm 103:13–17. He asked, 'Rico, what does this passage say about man, and what does it say about God?' I remember this so vividly. Verse 14 says, 'We are dust.' One day you will be able to hoover us up. I'll be a larger pile of dust than most of you, but we'll be hoovered up. What does it say about me in verse 15? Do you see? We may be dust, but actually we flourish for a short time like a flower of the field. And this nineteen-year-old picked up a bit of grass. We were on a mouldy old tennis court, and he said, 'Rico, we are blown away like grass.' My godfather had just been killed, and I knew that was true. Verse 16 says, 'and its place remembers it no more'. Think of your bedroom at home; think of the desk where you read. There'll be a day when no-one will know that you were in that place, your most precious place. I know what you are doing now: you are thinking, 'I'm going home and putting a plaque up.' No, 'its place remembers it no more'.

But what does verse 13 say about God?

> As a father has compassion on his children,
> so the LORD has compassion on those who fear him.

He said, 'Rico, that fear is like my fear of the sea. I love the sea, but I don't play games with the sea. I don't go thirty miles out to jump into it.' And then, verse 17 was the conversion verse for me:

> But from everlasting to everlasting
> the LORD's love is with those who fear him,
> and his righteousness with their children's children.

He said, 'Rico, God is forever, and if you link up with God, you'll live forever, so link up with God.' And at that moment it was as though God picked me up and I tore over the fence into eternity. That was a nineteen-year-old between sets of tennis with five minutes, five verses and two questions.

That's Bible sharing, and we've all got to do it. We can't just have it from the front – we are all to be Bible sharers; we all have this commission. So please don't tell me you don't know enough; we just need the boldness to obey and say, 'Would you like to look at the Bible with me? Have you looked at the documents for yourself?' And they can say 'yes' or 'no'. Brothers and sisters, in a culture that trusts authority less and less, people are only trusting friends – that's you, with your next-door neighbour, your colleague, your loved one.

The King's presence

We think, 'You know, I just don't think I can do it. I mean, I look at a command like this and I want to call in sick.' Well, wonderfully, there is a promise of the King's presence in verse 20: 'And surely I am with you always, to the very end of the age.' The constant presence of the Lord of mission is what makes mission possible. He is with us by his Spirit who lives in us and makes us one with him. O, his humility to abide in us and contend with us! Isn't that amazing? Where we are, so is Jesus. He asks great things of us, but he never asks us to do it alone. The Great Commission to go and make disciples of all nations (verse 19) is hedged by two of the most encouraging statements. If it were not for this, it would be too much. We'd say, 'We are not strong enough; we can't do it.' We couldn't bear the weight of responsibility. But we can do this, because the authority rests on the shoulders of Jesus Christ. He has taken responsibility himself (verse 18). So, when you ask someone to read the Bible with you, you do so with the authority of Jesus Christ risen from the dead. He gives you the right to ask; he gives you the right to go.

Secondly, I can only take on this vast responsibility of going to my neighbour, my work colleague, my friend, to the nations, in his name, because he is going to be with me. He says, 'Surely I am with you always, to the very end of the age' (verse 20). So, I wonder if you've got this, brother and sister: the King's victory, the most stupendous victory ever; death is conquered and the graveyards of the world are flung open; the King's authority over all nations; the King's seal, the sign of the cross uniting us with the universal fellowship and linking us with the local body; the King's commandment to 'Go' and the King's presence, 'I'll be with you always.' O, what world-changing words!

Note

1. C. S. Lewis, *Mere Christianity* (William Collins, 2012).

Living in the Power of the Trinity

by Peter Baker

Peter Baker became the Minister of Lansdowne Baptist in Bournemouth in June 2013. He is married to Sian, a BBC producer, and they have two daughters. Peter is Welsh, an Oxford history graduate and double blue. He has a passion for developing Christian leaders and in his spare time is a freelance religious broadcaster with the BBC.

Living in the Power of the Trinity: Ephesians 3:14–21

Larry Walters was a frustrated truck driver who wanted to be a pilot. The US Air Force turned down his application, but he never gave up his dream. One day he hit on a novel way of realizing his ambition to fly. He went to his local army surplus store and bought up their entire stock of forty-five weather balloons. He filled them with helium and tied them to a deckchair in his back garden, which he anchored to the bumper of his jeep. He armed himself with a six-pack of beer and a pellet gun so that he could burst a few balloons when he wanted to come down again. He sat in the chair and cut himself loose.

To his surprise, instead of gently floating upwards, the chair shot up into the air as if it was jet-propelled, and soon Larry Walters found himself way up high. He was there about six hours before he drifted into the approach to Los

Angeles International Airport. A rather bemused American Airlines pilot radioed the control tower to say that he'd just passed a man in a deckchair, armed with a gun, at 12,000 feet.

Fortunately for Mr Walters, who was by now heading out to sea, the pilot's report was taken seriously. A navy helicopter was scrambled; the crew lowered a rope and towed him back to safety. As the LA police were leading him away, someone asked Mr Walters why he'd done it. He replied, 'A man can't just sit around in a deckchair all day; he has to have his dreams.'

You've been sitting around a lot this week. You've heard lots of great Bible teaching, but what are your dreams? Let me introduce you to another man who had a dream. This dream was generated by a prayer gigantic in scope and vision. It has been described as one of the most glorious prayers in the entire Bible, and I can see why. Like all the most helpful prayers, it's trinitarian – it involves the plan of the Father, the passion of the Son and the power of the Spirit.

The plan of the Father (verses 14–15)

In Ephesians 3:1–11 Paul gives us an extraordinary exploration of what God is doing through the church. And that truth is the reason Paul falls before God in prayer, overwhelmed and wanting God to do more and more of the same in the lives of these Christians. Do you believe that God wants to do more in you and with your life, that he has more of his grace and power for you to experience? Or are you basically sitting in your deckchair, with low expectations, waiting for heaven? Well, here is a prayer to send you into orbit! A prayer about living in the power of the Trinity.

Paul has just caught a glimpse of something so extraordinary that he longs for its fulfilment. That extraordinary something is the Father's great plan, which he describes in Ephesians 3:10: 'His intent was that now, through the church, the manifold wisdom of God should be made known to the rulers and authorities in the heavenly realms.' What's the plan? That through the gospel, which brings the church into being, God demonstrates his wisdom to the spiritual world.

This was the good news which Paul himself had been commissioned to proclaim. Through faith in Christ, Jew and Gentile could find their place together in the kingdom of God. God was doing something so remarkable in the death and resurrection of Jesus, that the greatest enemies could be friends – those who had so little in common culturally would become part of the same family. And this divine plan is designed to be displayed to the heavens. God wants the watching world of angels to marvel at it. The history of the church is the graduate school of the angels. That's God's wisdom!

Now if you have been around church for any length of time, you might think it a rather foolish plan. Is God serious? How on earth can the church possibly be the demonstration of his wisdom? We know ourselves and our tendency to mess up, to beat each other up, and find each other impossible to work with and love. But that's the whole point. This is what makes the church so glorious. There is nothing like it. No tennis club, rotary society or old boys' association gets anywhere near what the church is. For, at its best, it is a display of the truth of God's grace.

When the lady in the pew with the expensive hat sits next to the man with the tattoo, nose rings and ripped jeans; when the posh accent is heard alongside slang; when the professor and the plumber study the Bible together because what they do is not half as important as who they are in Christ; when the people who really enjoy classical music rejoice when the next hymn is a drum and electric guitar fest; when the grandad is laughing with a student, and neither is bothered by their age because both of them are loved equally by God; when the regular church attendee approaches the newcomer standing alone and says, 'I don't know who you are, but you are welcome here' – that's the wisdom of God.

And God the Father says to the angels, 'See that, hear that – that's what my Son brings about. That's what the gospel can produce, the sort of society my love creates, that's my church.' That's what Paul means when he says in verse 15, 'from whom every family in heaven and on earth derives its name'. The Father creates the church, God gives us our identity, and nothing and nobody can take it away. For sure, we are not the church in heaven yet; we are the church on earth. So we're not all we should be, but we're not what we once were, and we're not yet all we're going to be. But to get there, to become all that God wants the church to be, we need the plan of the Father, but also:

The power of the Spirit (verses 16–17a)

Paul says, 'I pray that out of his glorious riches he may strengthen you with power through his Spirit in your inner being, so that Christ may dwell in your hearts through faith' (verses 16–17a). This prayer is a prayer for strength, for power. We'll see the purpose of this power in a moment.

First, consider the source of this power. Paul says the source is the Father's glorious riches. God the Father wants us to grasp his plan for the church to be the demonstration of his wisdom to the watching world. And for that to happen, he is going to equip us with all the resources and power we need to get the job done. So the Spirit brings to us the Father's glorious riches. Therefore there is nothing we are going to need that we haven't got in God in order to fulfil the plan. We are fabulously rich, amazingly resourced, and the Spirit brings that all into play.

But where is the power of God to stick with the plan located? Paul says in 'your inner being', 'the heart' (verse 17). On a Saturday afternoon as the rugby match is about to start on the TV, you often hear someone, usually Dad, shout, 'Where's the remote?' The remote controls everything – biblically, spiritually. For the remote control, think 'heart', and ask, 'Who's got my heart?' Jesus says that we can only give our heart to one person or one thing at a time.

It's the heart that needs to be strengthened, because it's there that the battle is won and lost for control. And God has all the resources we need to live a life of victory, a life of increasing peace and likeness to Christ, of living the adventure of faith. God has so much more for us: glorious riches to empower us so that we gain control of our hearts and live differently. And it's not shivers down the spine in worship that tell us we have the power, but God in my heart, living in me by his Spirit.

So, if the source is God's riches and the location is the heart, why does God want us to be strong there? What's the purpose of this internal power? Verse 17 says, 'so that Christ may dwell'. It's Christ in me. In the deepest parts of our lives, the interior world of motives and desires, it's all about the formation of a relationship. The Holy Spirit's agenda is to make us more like Christ. How does that happen? It happens when Christ by his Spirit dwells, takes up residence or occupation, in our heart. New Testament Greek has two words for a house or dwelling place. One is used for temporary accommodation – a student flat, a rented apartment for a week in Keswick, a bed and breakfast, or a tent by the lake. The other word is the one for a permanent home. Paul uses the second here. Jesus wants to live with us permanently, not as a lodger or tenant, but as a member of the house. But he cannot share the accommodation with pride, bitterness, impurity. If we want to entertain Christ, certain things will have to go.

The Holy Spirit has the power to change us so that we no longer want to have Jesus cohabiting with these things.

But for the house to be put in order, we need to go to him in faith and allow him access. We will never know his power otherwise. And because God gives to us out of his riches, he is able to meet our needs, to give us power to change and fill our homes with truth and purity. The Spirit works at 'closing the gap', so that what we are actually matches what we say. To have Christ in the heart is to have his Spirit in the heart. It is by the Spirit that Christ dwells in our hearts, and as he does so he gives strength. The more the Spirit empowers, the more Christ dwells in us, the more of the Spirit we know, the more of Christ we have.

The relationship goes deeper, and that takes us to the third feature:

The passion of the Son (verses 17b–19)

It is specifically the work of the Spirit's power in us to reveal to us how much we are loved by the Son. The only power that God is interested in is the power of love. And the greatest love in all the world is the love of God, revealed to us in the life, death and resurrection of Christ. The Spirit of Christ who dwells in us wants us to grasp the dimensions of his love for us.

So Paul prays for these Christians that they will be rooted and grounded in love, in order to know how much they are loved by a love that is so high, deep, long and wide, that no-one can ever know it fully. 'Rooted' is a botanical word. Love is the best soil in which people grow and develop: that is true in every relationship and walk of life. I can be all that I truly am when I know that I am loved. 'Grounded' is an architectural word. When my foundations are built upon the love of God to me in Christ, I will reach my potential in Christ.

On a recent visit to Seoul, South Korea, I had a conversation with Sam Ko, the Pastor of Global Missions at SaRang Church. He told me about the exciting new building which the church was a year from completing. It's going to cost them 300 million dollars and would be one of the tallest skyscrapers in that part of Seoul. He took me to see it. When I got to the site, there wasn't much there – just the very basic outline of the foundations sticking up at ground level. That's all. All the work that had been going on for the previous two years was underground. He explained, 'If you want to go high, then you must first go down deep.' That's how it is for us in the Christian faith. Do you want to know how high God's love is? Then be grounded in that love. Go deeper and then you can reach up higher.

I guess I've read verse 18 a thousand times before. But this time as I read it, one phrase stuck out: 'together with all the Lord's holy people'. If I want to know what the love of God is all about, I need the saints around me to show me. Of course, you can be a Christian without going to church, but you will never fully know what being a Christian is all about until you truly belong to a Christian community. Lone-Ranger Christians miss out on experiencing and understanding the love of God to them, because it's together that we see it and grasp it with fresh insight. It requires the whole people of God to make sense of the whole love of God.

So, as my roots grow deeper into God's love for me, I become stronger, more stable. And the stronger I become in that love, the more of that love I can know and experience. That's where Paul goes next in verse 19: 'and to know this love that surpasses knowledge – that you may be filled to the measure of all the fullness of God'. How can you know what can't be known? To those who know what love can do and how love can change us, it makes sense.

That's the offer on the table from God: to know his unknowable love in Christ. God wants us to know that we are loved by him, because when we know we're loved by God, we can become all that he wants us to be – 'filled to the measure'. And through knowing that we are loved by God, to the greatest extent that it is possible for a human being to be, we will become full of God's life, presence and power. We will be filled to capacity with as much of God as a human being can handle.

Now, I'm not there yet, and I doubt very much that you are. I'm not as full of God as Peter Baker can be. But that's what we are to be aiming for. And the key to it is knowing the love of Christ more and more as he dwells by faith in our hearts. What does that mean practically? It means more and more of God in our lives, cleansing our sins, healing our wounds, changing our attitudes, making us like Jesus. As I say, we are not there yet, but we will be one day. To be filled with all the fullness of God is possible perfectly and completely only in heaven. But – and here's where I went into orbit – Paul isn't praying for these people to know that then; he is praying for them to know that *now*! What a prayer to pray, that you and I be filled with the fullness of God *now*.

The prospect for the church (verses 20–21)

Is it possible for the Spirit of Jesus to so live in me that my heart belongs to him? Paul says in verses 20–21, 'Now to him who is able to do immeasurably more than all we ask or imagine, according to his power that is at work within us, to him be glory in the church and in Christ Jesus throughout all generations, for ever and ever! Amen.' So, can God really do that? Yes, he can and more, immeasurably more, than we ask or even dream. He can do it in us, the church, he can do it in every generation, from now on, and he will do it into eternity. You won't find that phrase 'immeasurably more' anywhere else in the New Testament. It's a virtually untranslatable super superlative. There are no limits to what God the Father can do through the power of the Spirit to form his Son in our hearts.

He can do immeasurably more because of his glorious riches. The Father's giving therefore can never exceed our capacity for asking or even imagining. Therefore ask on, dream on. But there's another resource: 'according to his power that is at work in us' (verse 20). This is no ordinary power. This is nothing less than the power that raised Jesus from the dead, now available in the life of the believer. Look at Ephesians 1:19–20: '... his incomparably great power for us who believe. That power is the same as the mighty strength he exerted when he raised Christ from the dead and seated him at his right hand in the heavenly realms.'

So we have all the wealth of heaven and all the power of God at work in us. Why? For what purpose? Is the 'immeasurably more' that God wants to do for us about our personal career agendas, the landing of a new job, a dream relationship, a bigger house? We tend to take that verse and wrap it around our desires for this or that. What's the purpose? The purpose is for God's glory in the church and in Jesus Christ. Without Christ, there would be no glory for us; every spiritual blessing comes to us through Christ. So, this glory is going to be in the church, but it's also going to be in Jesus, because when the church is glorified, Christ is glorified. It's a glory in time, in history, through all generations. However, its ultimate fulfilment will be in eternity, for ever and ever.

And it all begins with a request, a prayer: 'Lord, what do you want to do in my life, in my church? Am I in the way, resisting you, grieving your Spirit? Lord, strengthen me with the Spirit's power; overflow my life with your love. Help me clear out the rubbish in the house and give you the remote. Here I am, Lord; I want my life to count for your glory for ever.'

This can start here this evening, but our prayer will need to be repeated every day, as we open ourselves to the Father's plan, the Spirit's power and the Son's passion.

Keswick 2013

Keswick Convention 2013 Bible Readings,
Evening Celebrations and Lectures available free on www.keswickministries.org
Listen or download the mp3

Keswick Convention 2013 teaching from Essential Christian
All Bible readings and talks recorded at Keswick 2013 are available now on CD, DVD,* MP3 download and USB stick from www.essentialchristian.com/keswick.

Keswick teaching available as an MP3 download
Just select the MP3 option on the teaching you want, and after paying at the checkout your computer will receive the teaching MP3 download – now you can listen to teaching on the go: on your iPod, MP3 player or even your mobile phone.

Over fifty years of Keswick teaching all in one place
Visit www.essentialchristian.com/keswick to browse Keswick Convention Bible teaching as far back as 1957! You can also browse albums by worship leaders and artists who have performed at Keswick, including Stuart Townend, Keith & Kristyn Getty, plus Keswick Live albums and the *Precious Moments* collection of DVDs.

To order, visit www.essentialchristian.com/keswick or call 0845 607 1672.

*Not all talks are available on DVD.

KESWICK MINISTRIES

Keswick Ministries is committed to the deepening of the spiritual life in individuals and church communities through the careful exposition and application of Scripture, seeking to encourage the following:

Lordship of Christ – to encourage submission to the lordship of Christ in personal and corporate living
Life Transformation by Word and Spirit – to encourage a dependency upon the indwelling and fullness of the Holy Spirit for life transformation and effective living
Evangelism and Mission – to provoke a strong commitment to the breadth of evangelism and mission in the British Isles and worldwide
Discipleship – to stimulate the discipling and training of people of all ages in godliness, service and sacrificial living
Unity and Family – to provide a practical demonstration of evangelical unity

Keswick Ministries is committed to achieving its aims by:

- providing Bible-based training courses for youth workers and young people (via Root 66) and Bible Weeks for Christians of all backgrounds who want to develop their skills and learn more
- promoting the use of books, DVDs, CDs and downloads so that Keswick's teaching ministry is brought to a wider audience at home and abroad

- producing TV and radio programmes so that superb Bible talks can be broadcast to you at home
- publishing up-to-date details of Keswick's exciting news and events on our website so that you can access material and purchase Keswick products on-line
- publicizing Bible teaching events in the UK and overseas so that Christians of all ages are encouraged to attend 'Keswick' meetings closer to home and grow in their faith
- putting the residential accommodation of the Convention Centre at the disposal of churches, youth groups, Christian organizations and many others, at very reasonable rates, for holidays and outdoor activities in a stunning location

Our vision is the spiritual renewal of God's people for his mission in his world.

If you'd like more details, please look at our website (www.keswickministries.org) or contact the Keswick Ministries office by post, email or telephone as given below.

Keswick Ministries
Convention Centre
Skiddaw Street, Keswick
Cumbria CA12 4BY

***Tel:* 017687 80075**
***email:* info@keswickministries.org**
follow us on Twittter @KeswickC

Keswick 2014

Week 1: 12th – 18th July
Week 2: 19th – 25th July
Week 3: 26th July – 1st August

The annual Keswick Convention takes place in the heart of the English Lake District, an area of outstanding national beauty. It offers an unparalleled opportunity to listen to gifted Bible exposition, meet Christians from all over the world and enjoy the grandeur of God's creation. Each of the three weeks has a series of morning Bible readings, and then a varied programme of seminars, lectures, prayer meetings, concerts and other events throughout the day, with evening meetings that combine worship and teaching. There is also a full programme for children and young people, with a programme for young adults during each week. Prospects will again be running a series of meetings for those with learning difficulties in Week 2. In Week 3 Keswick Unconventional brings an opportunity to explore more creative and imaginative aspects of Christian spirituality.

The theme for Keswick 2014 is

Really? Searching for Reality in a Confusing World

In a world of so many competing truth claims, is it really possible to find ultimate reality? Across all three weeks, we'll be hearing superb Bible teachers and apologists strengthening our conviction that ultimate reality can be found – and *is* really found – in the person of the Lord Jesus Christ.

In Week 3 2014 we'll be doing something new: crafting a programme that will be helpful to both convinced Christians *and* their non-Christian friends and family. The adult sessions that week will be slightly less busy and slightly more flexible, with chances throughout the day and in various settings for Christians to take their friends to attractive, appropriate events. The youth and children's tracks will be ready to welcome a higher-than-average number of youngsters from unchurched homes.

Of course, Conventioners who come to Week 3 without non-Christian friends can still expect spirit-refreshing, faith-strengthening Bible teaching and training that will be particularly helpful in equipping us to share the gospel more effectively back home. All the weeks of Keswick 2014 are for everyone, but start thinking and praying now; do you know friends or neighbours or family who don't yet know the Lord who could join you at Keswick 2014 Week 3? Who might love coming on holiday with you to this beautiful part of God's world – and at the same time hear God's beautiful good news?

The Bible readings will be given by:
Vaughan Roberts (Week 1)
Jonathan Lamb (Week 2)
Chris Sinkinson (Week 3)

Other confirmed speakers are Ivor Poobalan, Becky Manley Pippert, Richard Cunningham, Ruth Padilla de Borst, Ian Coffey, Ravi Zacharias, Roger Carswell and Michael Ramsden.*

* Speakers' list correct at time of going to press. Check out the website for further details.